Artwork
of
Charlotte W. Throop

James A. Shaw, MD

Copyright © 2018: James A. Shaw, MD

All rights reserved.

ISBN-10: 1985636301
ISBN-13: 978-1985636309

Cover Credit : The cover is a photographic reproduction of Charlotte W. Throop's art album: 1877 & 1879

CreateSpace Independent Publishing Platform

IN MEMORY OF

Charlotte W. Throop
(1829-1899)

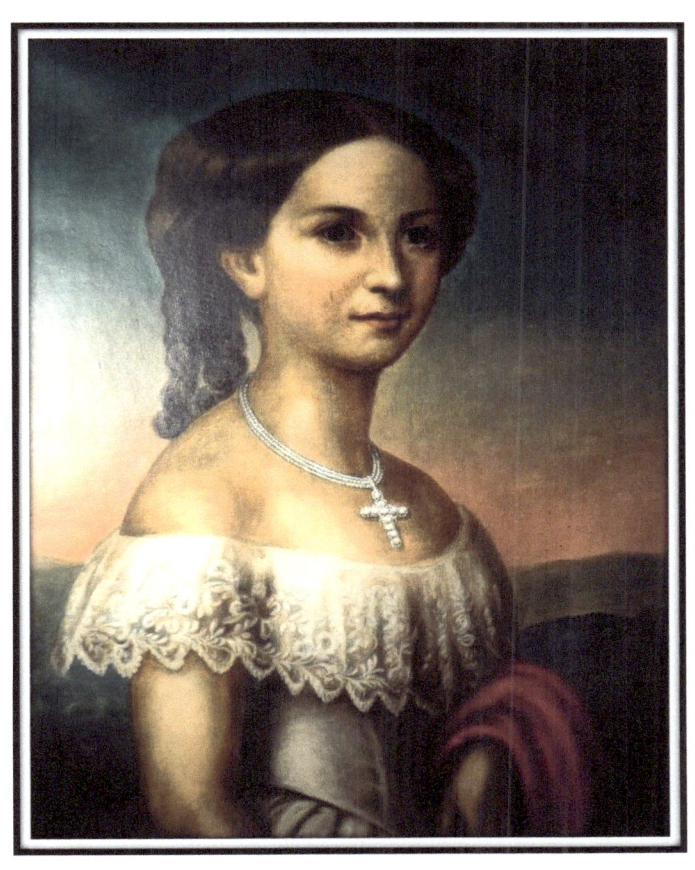

CONTENTS

1. Note to Readers — 7

2. Florals by Charlotte W. Throop — 11

3. Landscapes by Charlotte W. Throop — 73

4. Sketches by Montgomery H. Throop I — 77

Artwork

Note to Readers

Dear Readers,

    Charlotte Williams Gridley was born on June 17, 1829 in Hamilton, NY. Her father, Philo Gridley, was thirty-two years old and her mother, Susan Williams Gridley, was twenty-five at the time. Charlotte was the second of five girls born to the Gridley parents: An older sister Catherine was born in 1827; a sister, Cornelia, in 1832; another sister, Caroline, in 1933; and, finally, a fourth sister, Mary, in 1936.

    Charlotte's mother was born on June 3, 1804 in Waterville, NY and her father on September 16, 1796 in Paris, NY. Her father was a graduate of Hamilton College, studied law and was admitted to the bar in 1820 at age twenty-four. He married Susan Williams, the mother of his five girls, on May 20, 1826. In 1829 he was elected district attorney for Madison County and in 1846 he was elected a justice of the NYS Supreme Court, where he served from 1847-1853. He died August 16, 1864, having served in his retirement on the board of Hamilton College for many years. Charlotte's mother died on May 15, 1881 in Utica, NY at age seventy-six years.

    Unfortunately, very little is recorded in the historical record about Charlotte's mother, other than her role as a wife and mother. The same can be said about Charlotte, herself. What is known is that she married Montgomery Hunt Throop (1827-1892) on June 22, 1854 when she was twenty-five years old, assuming Charlotte W. Throop as her married name. Her husband studied law under his uncle, U.S. Supreme Court Justice Ward Hunt, and became a very prominent attorney and legal author about whom virtually everything can be learned with a click on the internet.

Charlotte and her husband had two children, the first being Montgomery Hunt (II), born March 22, 1856. A second son, Philo Gridley, born April 10, 1860, died in 1873 at the tender age of thirteen. After graduation from Columbia University (1876) and an inauspicious early career in journalism, Montgomery Hunt (II) studied for Holy Orders and became an ordained Episcopal priest in 1882, a calling which he later abandoned in 1899 in favor of the "entertainment business". His marriage in 1884 to Agnes Campbell (1856-1936) gave Charlotte and her husband two grandchildren, Montgomery Hunt (III) and Charlotte Agnes Throop. A third child, John Campbell, died in infancy.

The marriage between Montgomery Hunt (II) and his wife Agnes Campbell Throop, dissolved around 1897, at which point Agnes and her two young children, Montgomery Hunt (III) and Charlotte Agnes, went to live with her mother-in-law, Charlotte W. Throop, in Albany, NY. (Charlotte's husband, Montgomery H. Throop (I), had died a few years earlier, in 1892.) About 2 years later Charlotte died, leaving her entire estate to her daughter-in-law and in trust to her grandchildren, forgoing her son completely.

That is about all that is known about Charlotte W. Throop. Like most women of the time, her recorded life is focused on her husband and children and, in her case, serving as de facto guardian and financial benefactor of her daughter-in-law and two young grandchildren, all having been abandoned by her son.

No doubt, during much of her life, Charlotte assumed the role of solicitous wife and gracious host, consistent with societal expectations of the times. Based on the disposition of her estate, it is abundantly clear that she was a woman of generosity and compassion. **But what is unheralded by recorded history, is the fact that she was also a very talented artist!**

I am fortunate to have inherited a small album containing the floral artwork of Charlotte W. Throop from my mother, who was the great granddaughter of Charlotte W. Throop and her namesake. The album contains watercolor renditions of flowers observed by Charlotte on countryside carriage rides and hikes in Switzerland (and Scotland) during the summers of 1877 and 1879, mostly in the vicinity of Pontresina, Switzerland.

The album is decrepit and literally falling apart. The pictures are, in many cases, stained and weathered; but, despite the travails of 130 years, continue to show Charlotte's remarkable talent. Multiple paintings have been removed from the album, as evidenced by glue-scars and fade marks, no doubt by admiring relatives or friends who "borrowed" a sample for their own enjoyment. Some of the missing pictures have retained descriptions, which I have included in the narrative. Of concern, all remaining paintings need restoration and appropriate preservation.

As an interim step in preserving her work for posterity, I have photographed the pictures with a point-and-shoot camera and assembled them into this little book in an inexpert attempt to give them extended life, before they crumble to dust. Included are a couple of sketches by Charlotte's husband, Montgomery Hunt Throop (I), also a decent artist, which are pasted onto the back pages of Charlotte's album. Additionally, I have included two of Charlotte's Switzerland landscapes, which have been in my possession for many years, presumably painted during the same time period.

The flower names and dates are inscribed at the bottom of all the original paintings in Charlotte's cursive scrawl. Many of these inscriptions made cropping of worn and frayed painting edges difficult, so are included as typed text below the painting photographs in this book. A few examples of paintings with the original inscriptions are included for an element of authenticity. In some cases, the dates inscribed on the paintings suggest a non-sequential order within the album, but I have reproduced them in the sequence in which they appear.

Most of the floral images in this book are approximately two-thirds of their original size, not counting the painting's margins which were cropped for ease of presentation. The two landscapes are about half-size in both height and width. The album, itself, measures 7.5 x 9.5 inches.

What is obvious from the paintings and their accompanying descriptions is that Ms. Throop loved the outdoors, reveled in exploration and adventure, drew fortitude from the natural world and was inspired to paint by the beauty of flowers. A remarkable woman in many regards.

Charlotte W. Throop died in Albany, NY on the same day as her birth in 1899, at age 70 years. Her album has been donated to the New York State Library/Manuscripts and Special Collections, Albany, NY, and may be viewed by appointment.

Do enjoy,

James A. Shaw
Great, great grandson of Charlotte W. Throop

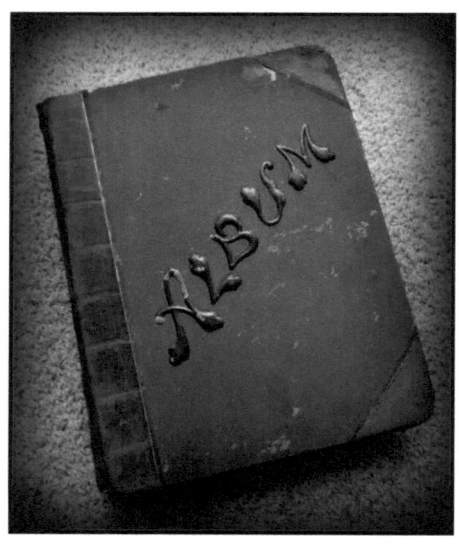

FLORALS
BY
CHARLOTTE W. THROOP

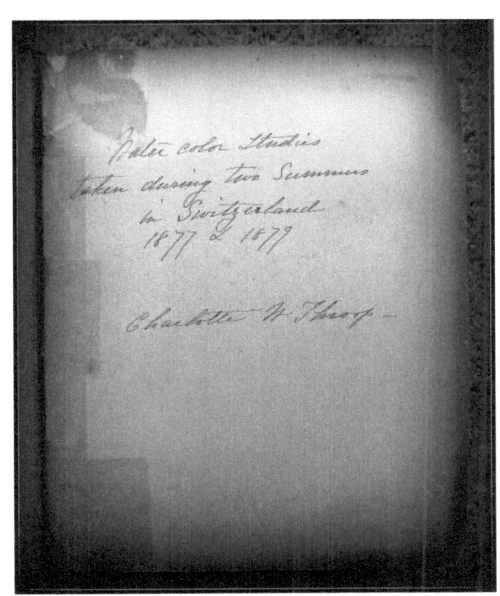

June 27, '77

The broom is a flowering shrub growing to 6 feet high or more. The Scotch called it "Whim", and a proverb of the country people implies that it is always in flower. This sprig was plucked during a drive through Queen's Park in Edinburg [Scotland] and around the Salisbury Craig and Arthur's Seat.

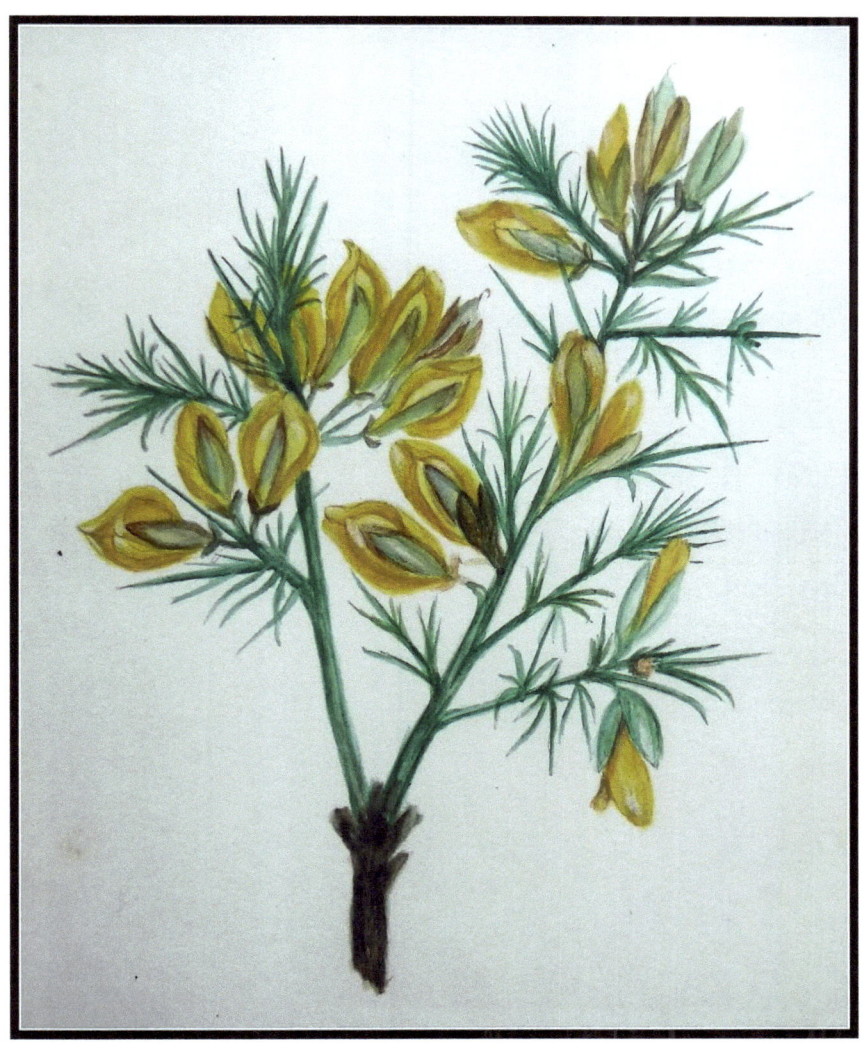

The Gorse (Scotch, "Whim") gathered in the Queen's Park at Hollyrood. June 27, 1877.

June 27, '77

These sweet Scotch daisies I gathered in the grass growing where once was the floor of the chapel at Hollyrood Palace. The chapel is in a ruin, but the palace is in a good state of preservation and the different rooms of Mary Queen of Scots pointed out, as well as the stain of Rizzo's [? Sp.] blood on the floor where he was murdered.

Artwork

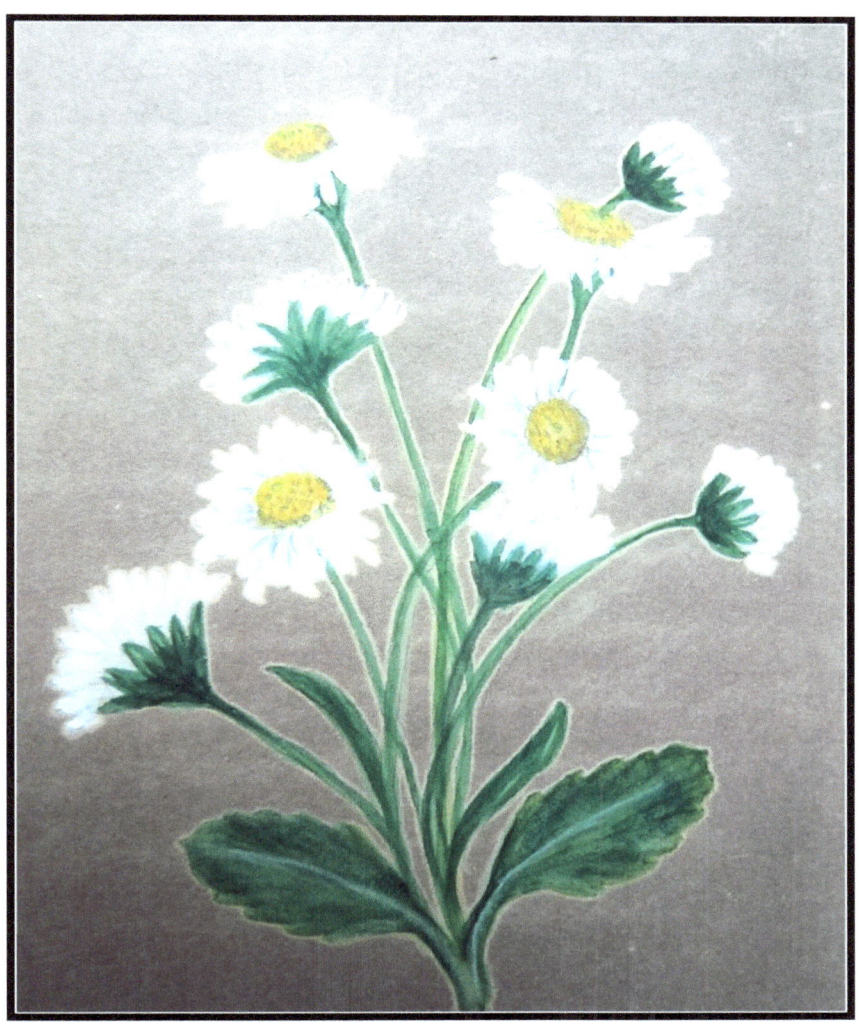

The Scottish daisy gathered June 27, 1877 growing in the ruined chapel at Hollyrood.

July 12, 1877

This bit of moss and flowers was gathered at Schaffhausen, the falls of the Rhine, one of the most charming spots in all one's summering. We arrived just after a thunderstorm, and sitting on that luxurious piazza was a capital dinner spread before us, champagne and all; drank in the beauty of the falls, the river and wooded banks, while the most perfect rainbow I ever saw spanned the whole scene. The flowers grew on a hillside in the grounds of the hotel.

Artwork

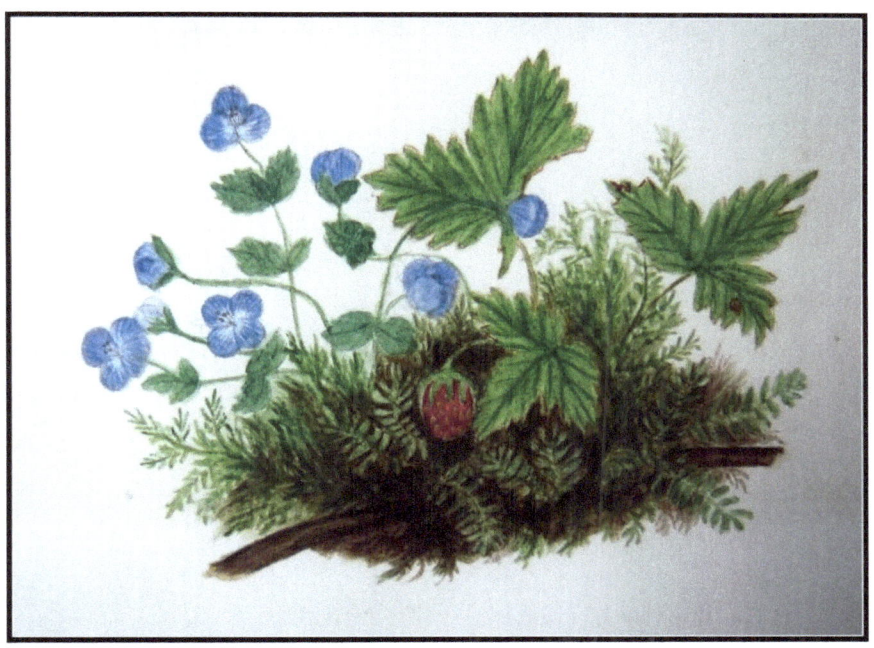

Veronica, moss and flowers gathered at Schaffhausen Rhine Falls. July 12, 1877

July 17, 1877

These harebells grew out of a stone garden wall with apparently no earth for their roots — and were pulled in a large handful by our driver as we slowly started up a long hill from Coire - on it two days' journey over the Alberta Pass into the Engadin. Coire (French) or Chur (German) is a most interesting place being at the terminus of the railway. [With] diligence [one] makes the journey over the pass in one day, but only by starting at 4 o'clock in the morning.

Artwork

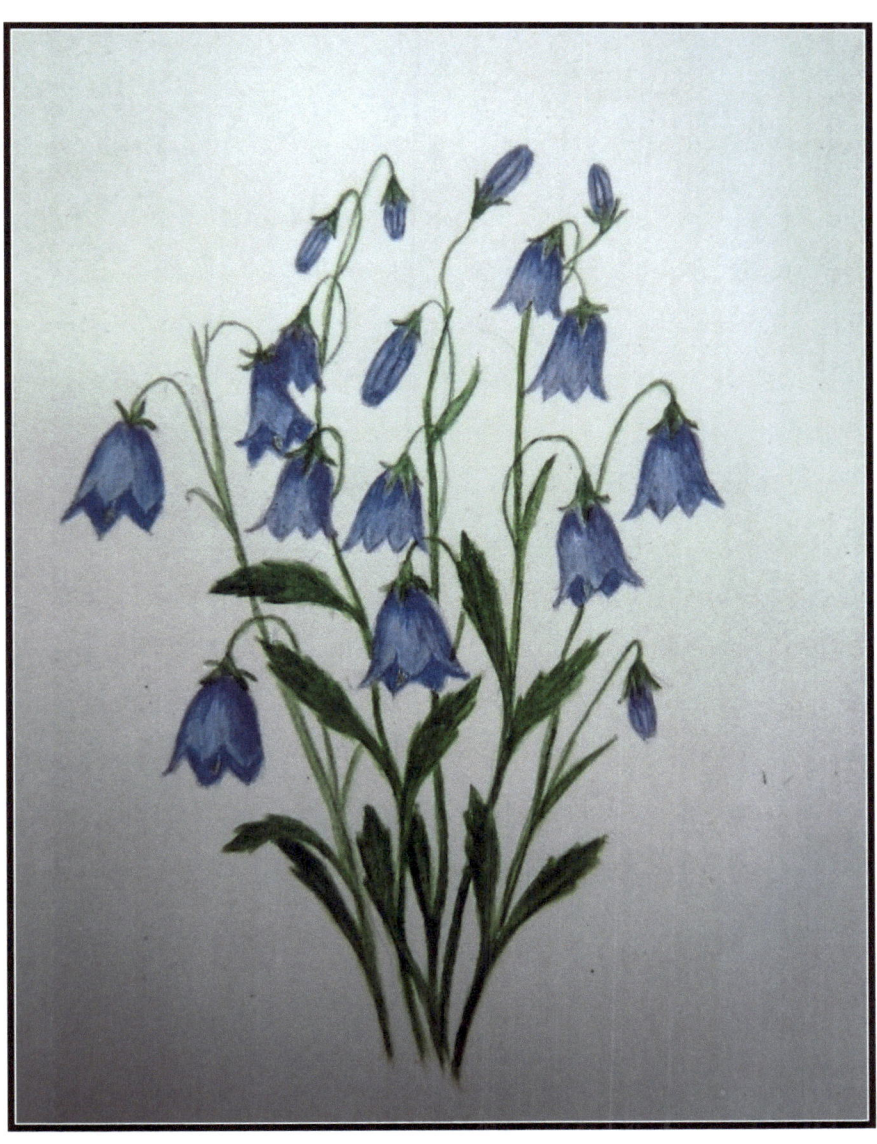

Blue Harebells gathered from the stone wall. Coire. July 17th

July, 1877

We left Bergen at eight in the morning with three horses and went up into and above the clouds. I had thought it much to see the snow peaks coming almost to a level with us, or we to them rather, but now we wound right in among them and our road passed through a cutting where the solid snow rose up in walls either side of us, from 6 to 8 feet high. We could not see over them by standing up in the carriage — and still flowers! Not actually on the snow, but close to it, as some of the snow ended and there was a little bit of earth on the rocks where there were beautiful wildflowers growing and there I gathered these pinks and pansies at the hospice nearly 8000 feet above sea level.

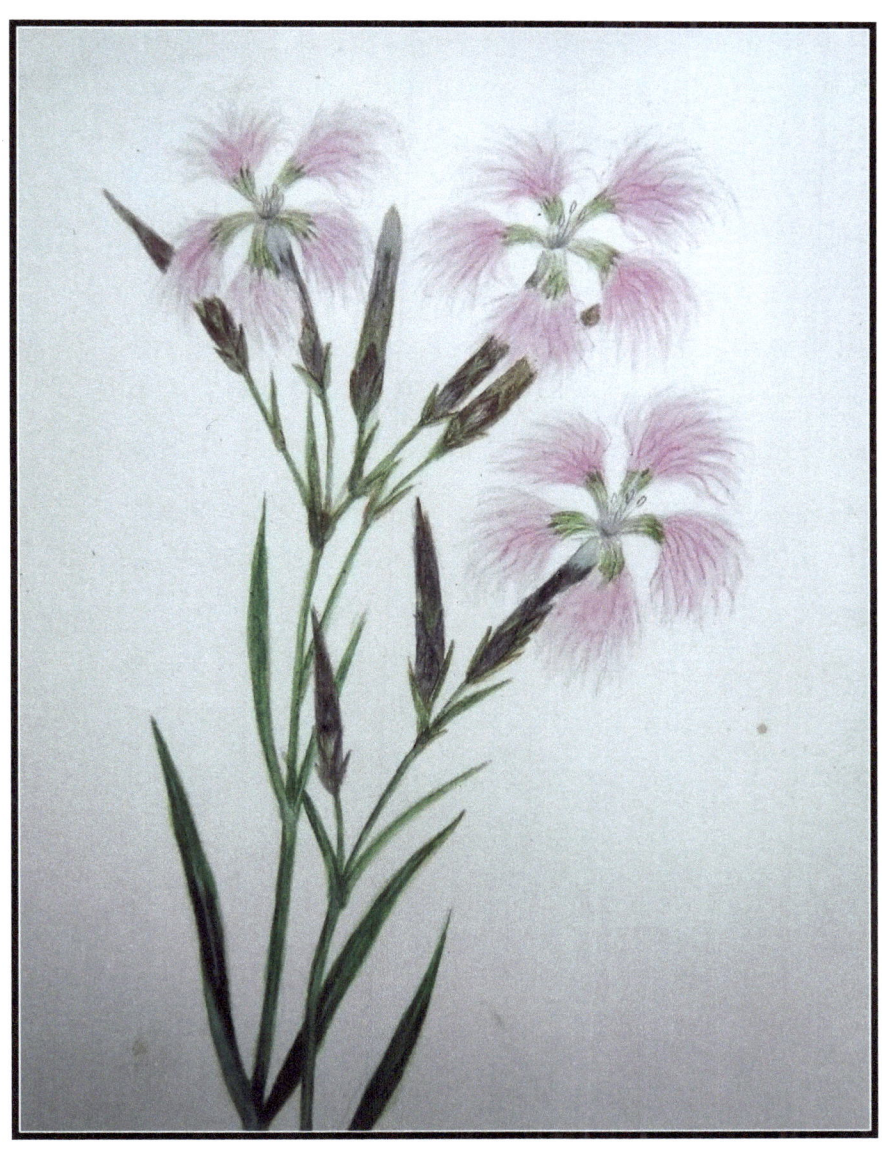

Pinks gathered on the Albula Pass. 5000 feet above the sea level. July 17, 1877

July, 1877

We had flurries of snow in our faces but we hailed them with glee and laughter for the sun was shining and we were wrapped in our furs. I cannot describe the sublimity and the majesty of that scene — for an hour on the highest part of the pass — all rocks and desolation; and yet not desolate, but grand with an ethereal majesty. On the top among the debris of huge rocks [was] a limped green lake; its surface moved by the breeze into innocent ripples. It seemed as if it hardly belonged to this world. The awe was intense. One could not talk. The whole place seemed to say: "Be still and know that I am God."

Artwork

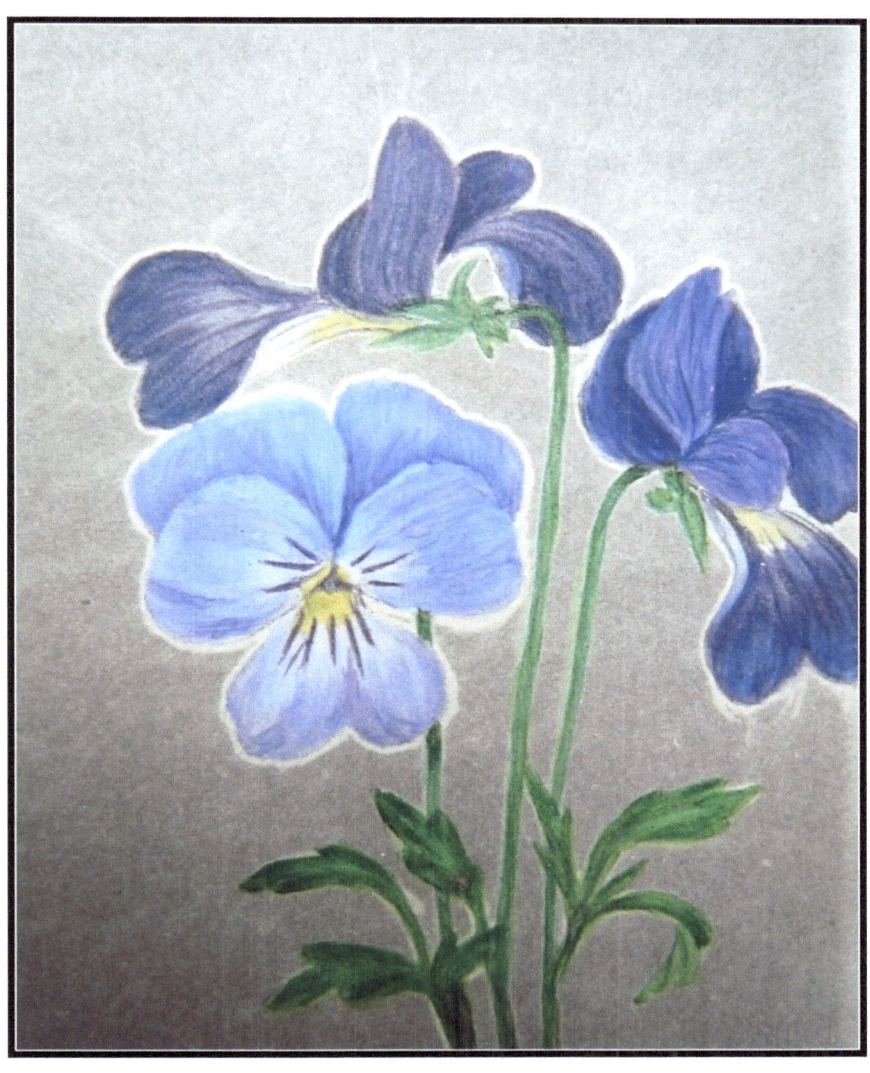

Wild pansies gathered on top of the Albula Pass. 7500 feet above the sea level by the hospice. July 18, 1877

Thursday July 26, 1877

"Ye shall go out with joy; and be led forth with peace. All the hills shall break forth before you into singing and the trees of the field shall clap their hands." Isaiah 45th, last verse. So it is in Pontresina, the gem of the Engadin— not in itself, but in its views and possibilities of walks and drives; from which one comes in late with the brilliant Alpine rose, gathered from every rock and also the delicate Tulphin Anemone, more difficult to find.

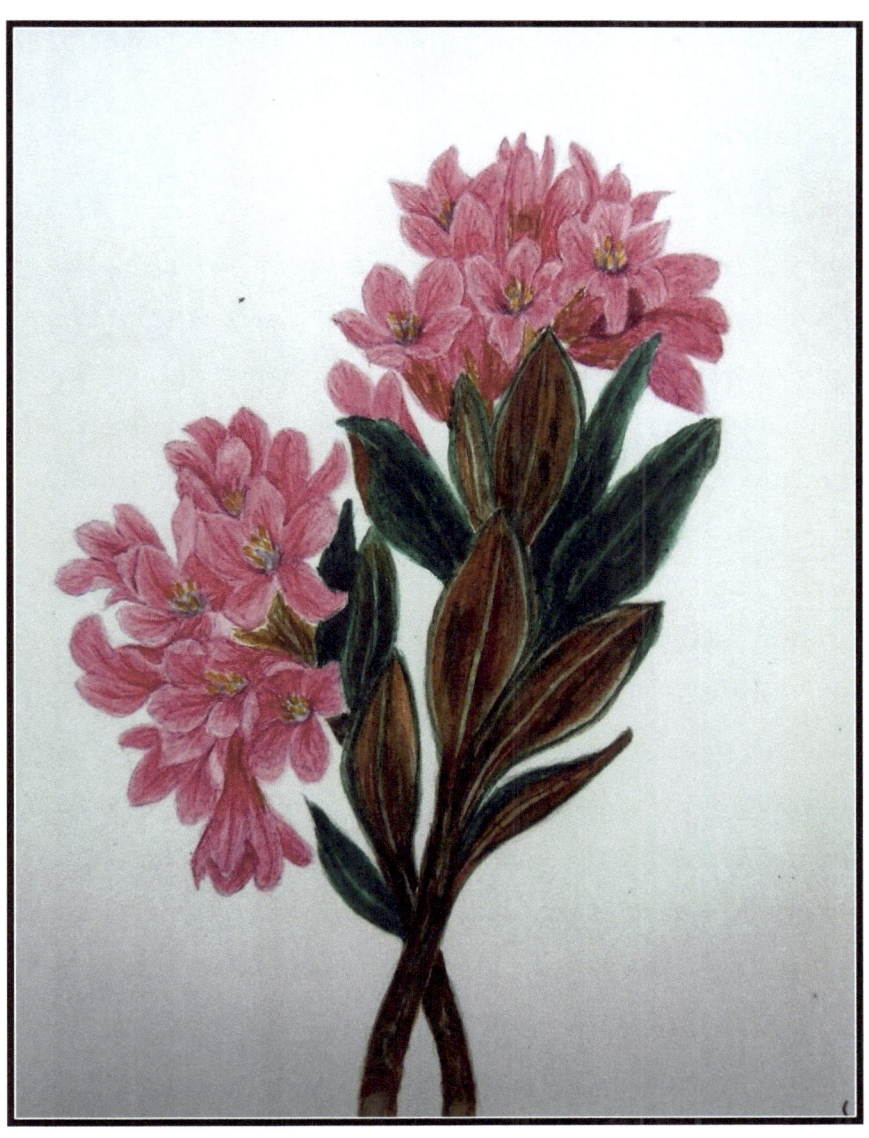

The Alpine rose or Rhododendron ferrugineum. Pontresina, Engadin. July 23.

Pontresina — July 30th.

I am ready to write now, for I have been charmed all day. We had a fire to get up and dress by, which made today start with comfort. The glacier is so beautiful that I begrudged to leave it and go to drive, as we did, to St. Moritz and to [?]. Neither of them can compare with our situation. Roseg glacier is so glorious. Tonight the sunset on it with the full moon risen above it. All day it has been a pearl of purest sheen and tonight a pale ruby glistening. Ladies have bought me flowers to sketch from their rambles. This Daphna grows low over the rocks and smells as sweet as our lilac blossoms. We walked through the valley on the other side of the river, up in the woods where I gathered the roses and innumerable other flowers. It was exquisite over there among the rocks and mosses and flowers with the great mountains towering up on every side, standing out clear cut against the blue sky and every summit glistening with snow.

Artwork

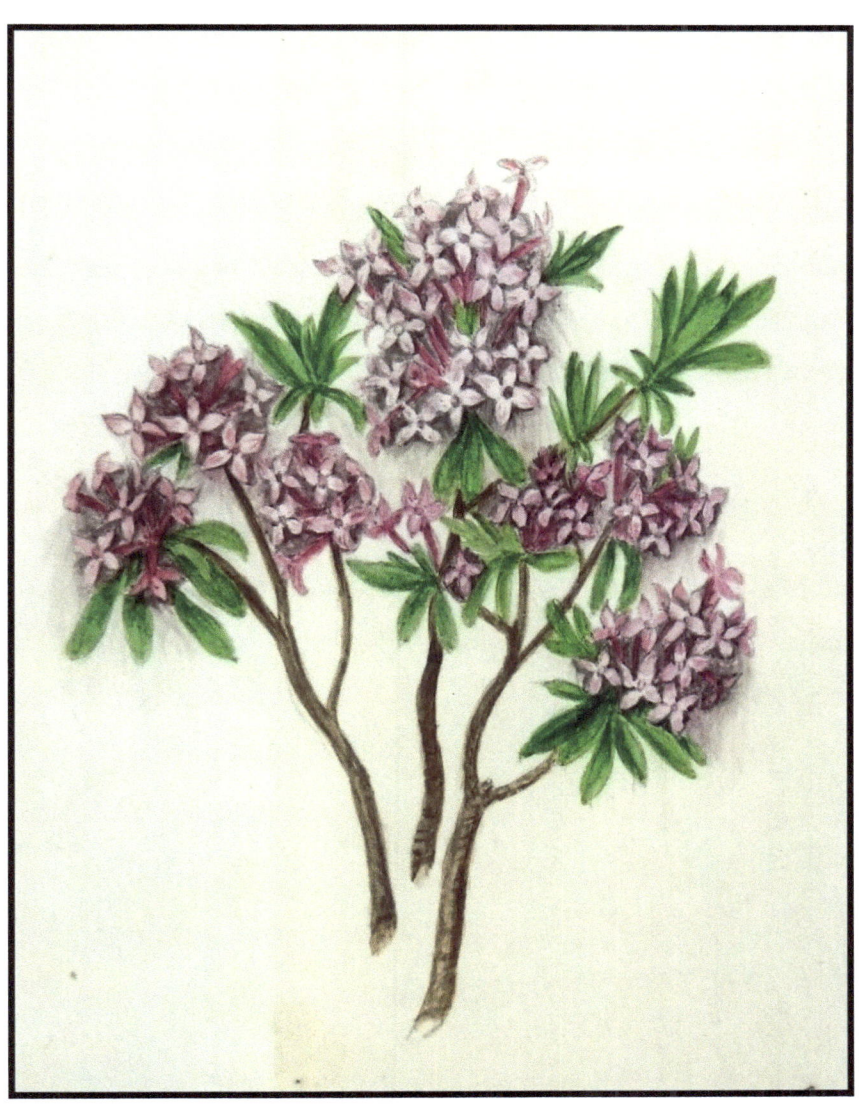

The Daphna from Mount Schaffburg. July 30, 1877.

July 31, 1877

The mountains magnificent, ever-changing in sun and shade. The valley a scene of fertile beauty. The crowds of Italian haymakers fill the air with the scent of new mown hay. We crossed the lower bridge among them and walked up the other side of our river [indecipherable] above "Point [indecipherable]" to the bank where the Linnea Borealis covers the ground with its network of vines with its tiny pink bells ringing the fairies to their dance in this dancing sunshine. Down deep below we can see the white foam of the river rushing through the gorge fighting with the opposition of the narrow passage between the cliffs.

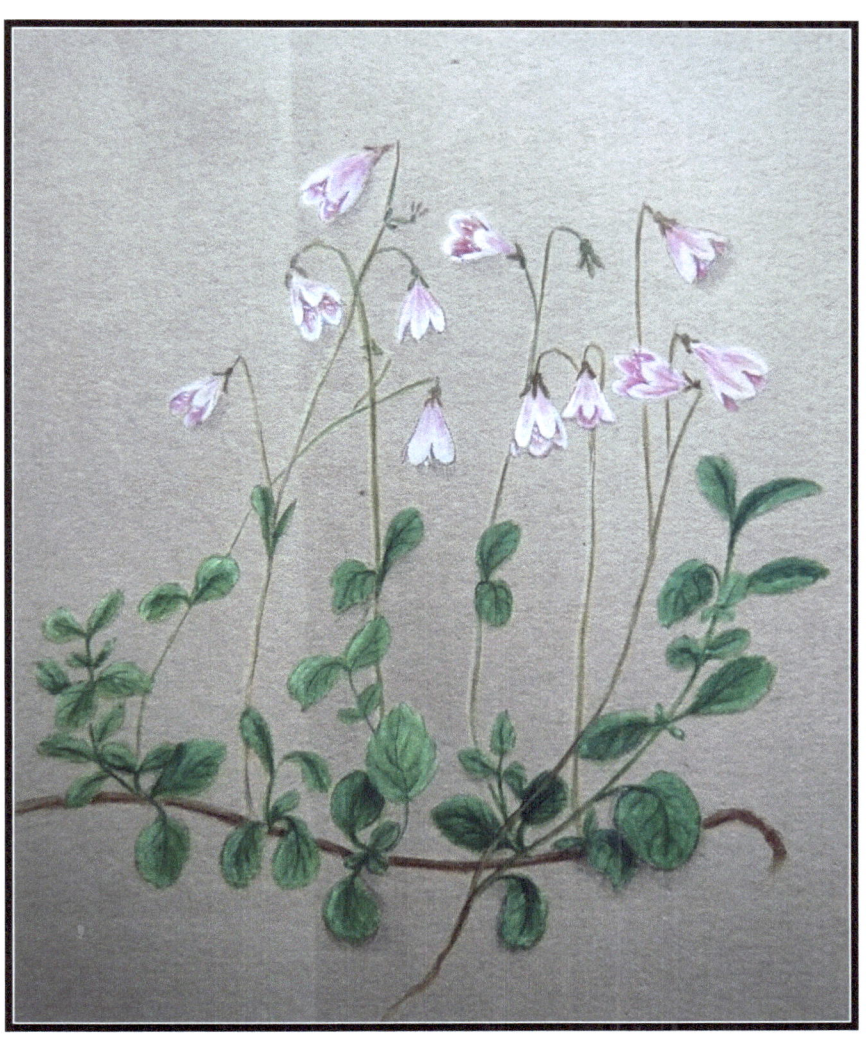

The Linnaea Borealis. Pontresina. August 1, '77

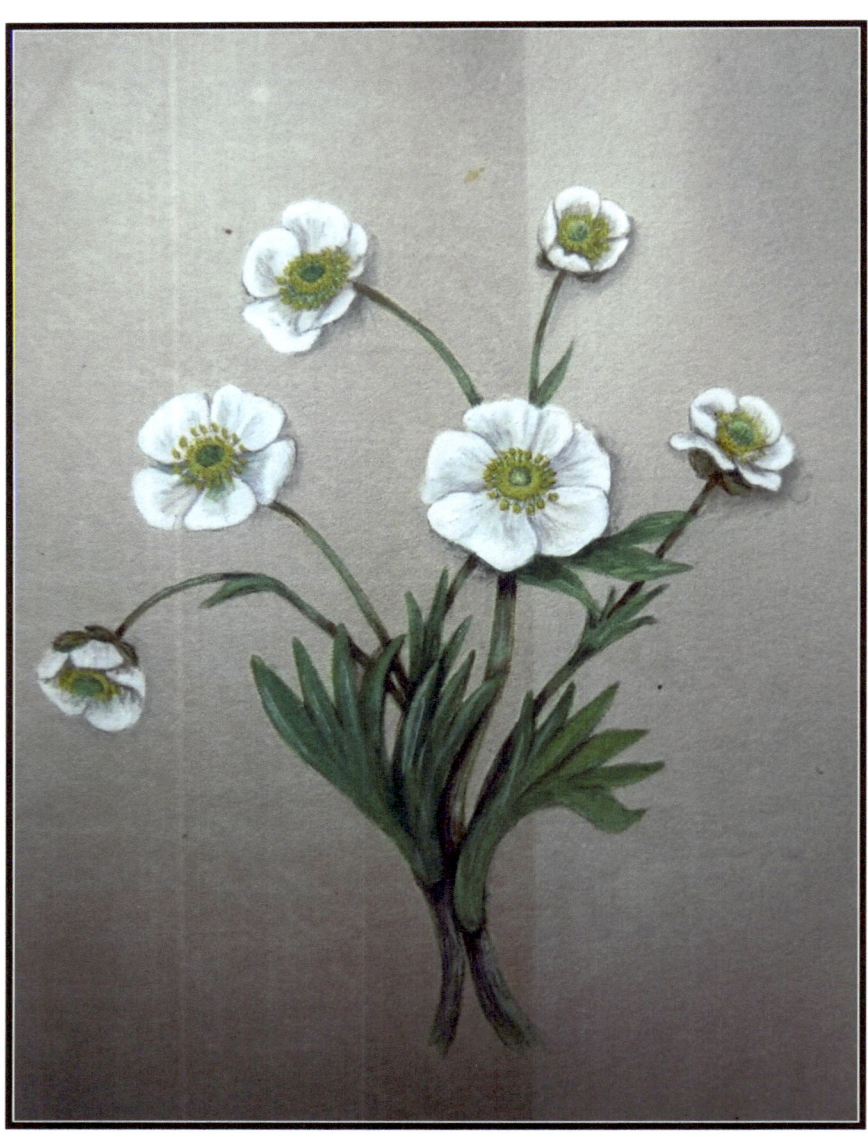

Ranunculus glacialis. Bernina pass. Aug 4th, '77

July 31, 1877

We have been up the Roseg valley today with friends. Other carriages proceeded ours and the people started off on their walk up the Alp Ota, where I intended to go. Those in our carriage knew no more of the route than I did, and we made the mistake of not seeing where the path turned off up the mountainside, and so continued walking up the valley until we arrived at the moraine of the glacier. I knew then that we had mistaken the path and returned the 3 miles, but my friends had brought me a lily to paint, as well as some of the precious Edelweiss which is getting scarce now even in the Alps.

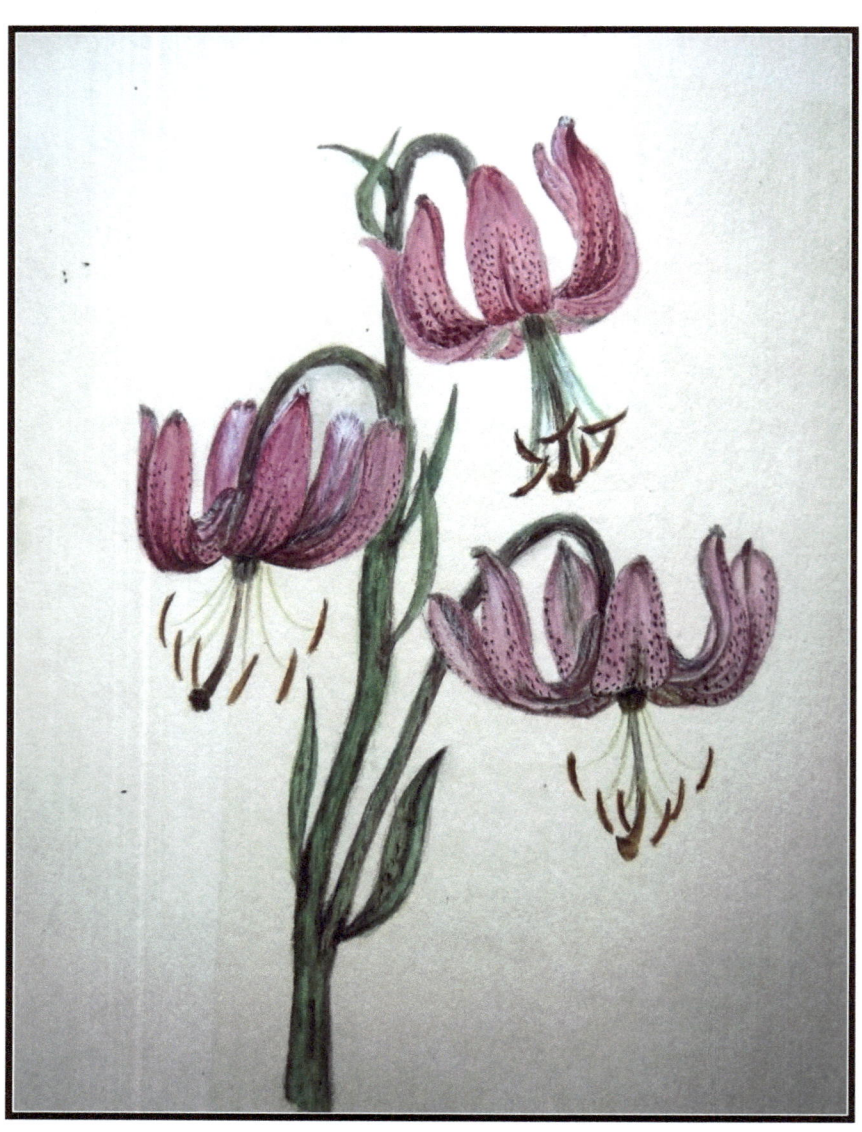

Lily from Alp Ota. Aug 8th, '77

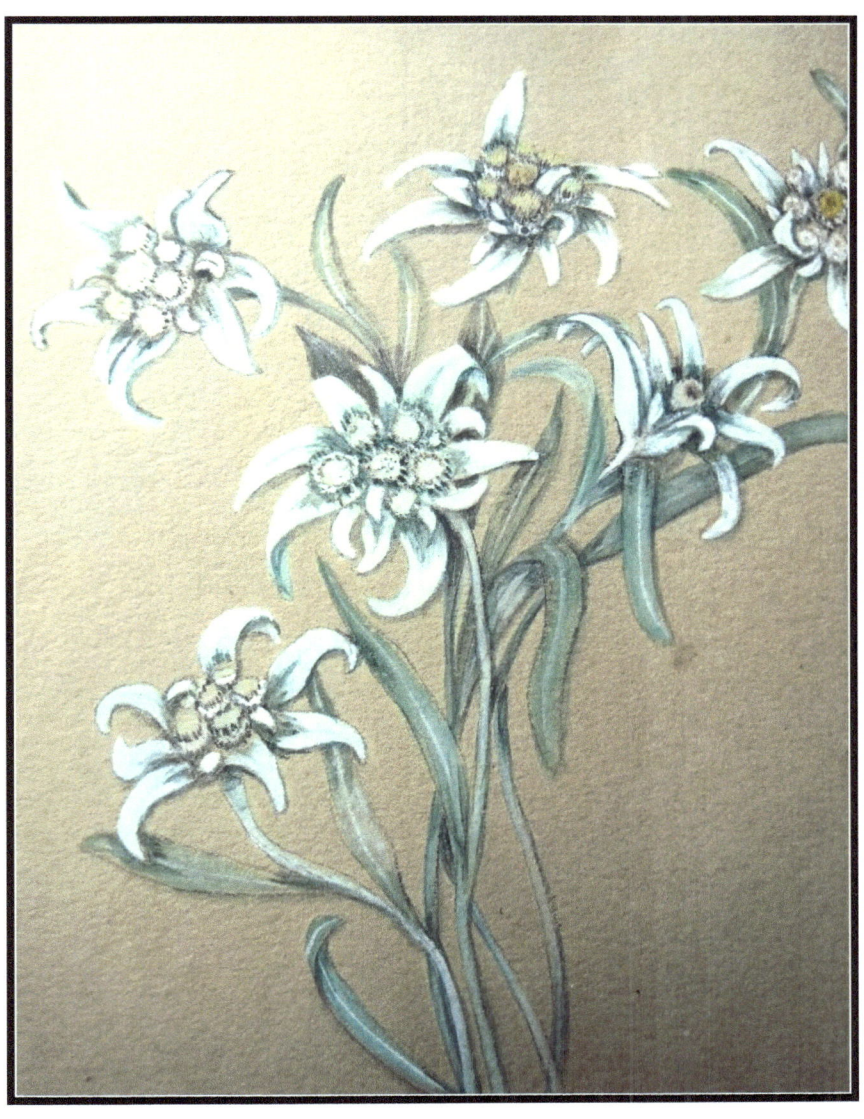

Edelweiss, Alp Ota, Roseg valley. August 79

August 3, 1877

We have been on a long walk today up to the old [Spaniola] tower and the little church abandoned now, of the 14th century — touching with the grave yard about it, all the inscriptions in Romansh. The tower dates from the 10th century. It is very strong, five sided, thick stone walls with no entrance lower than about 20 feet high — they must have entered by ladders. It is supposed to be a remnant of a castle built by the [indecipherable], who overran this country. There grow these beautiful pink roses — true Sweet briar, with different foliage and perfume from the common wild rose of the country, which is red.

Artwork

[Two Missing Paintings]

Aug, 1877

We have come in from the long and charming walk around the old [Spaniola] tower, five sided with no entrance lower than 20 feet or so from the ground. All this country is so interesting, having been settled at first by the [? Sp.] and having many of their ruins – mosque shaped domes, etc. After a ramble through the words on the mountainside we came in laden with "forget-me-nots" which grow in such abundance, pink as well as blue, so that one gets a bunch as large as one's head in a few minutes.

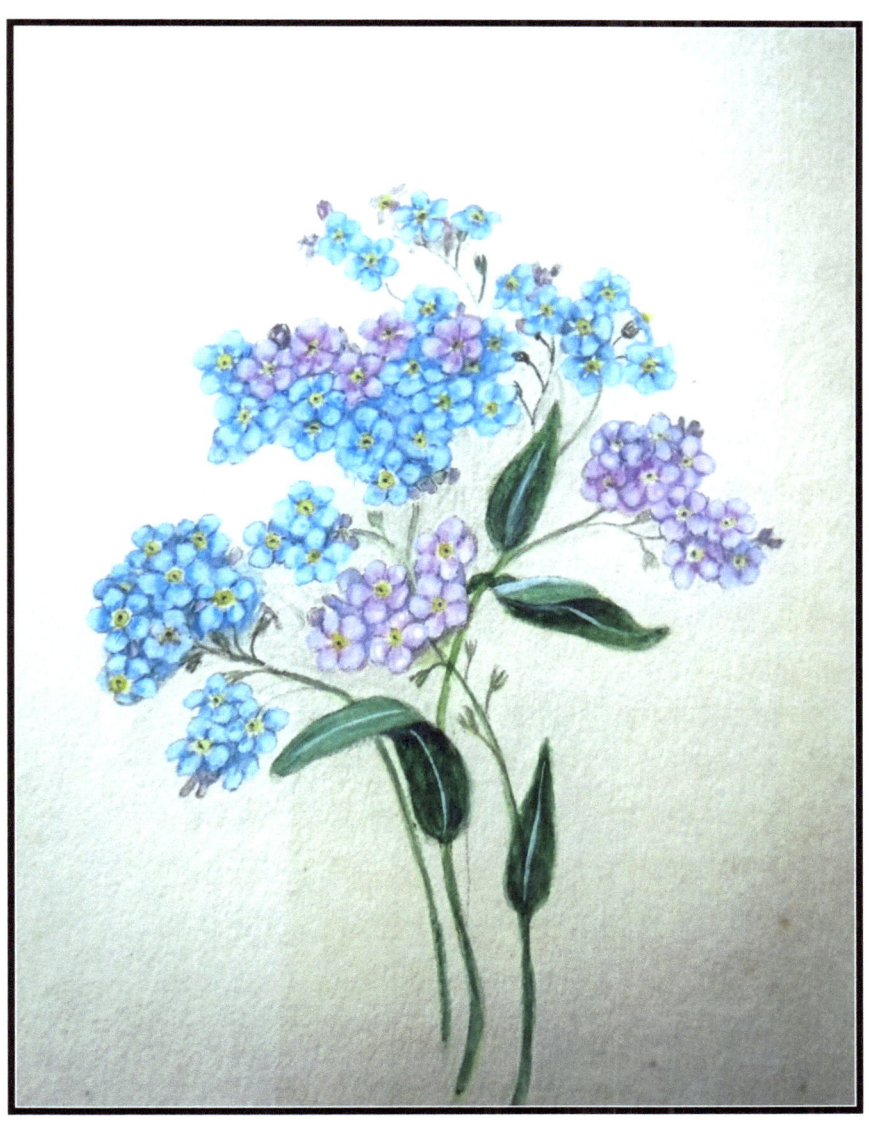

"Forget-me-not" of the high Alps – pink and blue. Pontresina, Aug. 18.

Aug., 1877

I had been to the top of Mt. Schafberg that afternoon, so after dinner I went to bed when M. [Montgomery] came in and said our friend, the old English officer, was coming in to bid us goodbye. I got up and dressed again to receive him. He has been so kind to bring me flowers from every inaccessible place. This very afternoon, while M. was resting, he had come in to leave some for me. The purple flower on a tall stem he put by itself in a glass and, not seeing anyone on the bed, he stepped back gazing at it in apparent rapture and clapped his hands softly and left it. I inquired the next day of English friends who all know so much about flowers and botany. They told me it was "Soldenella" [?] and the flower that [indecipherable] raves about.

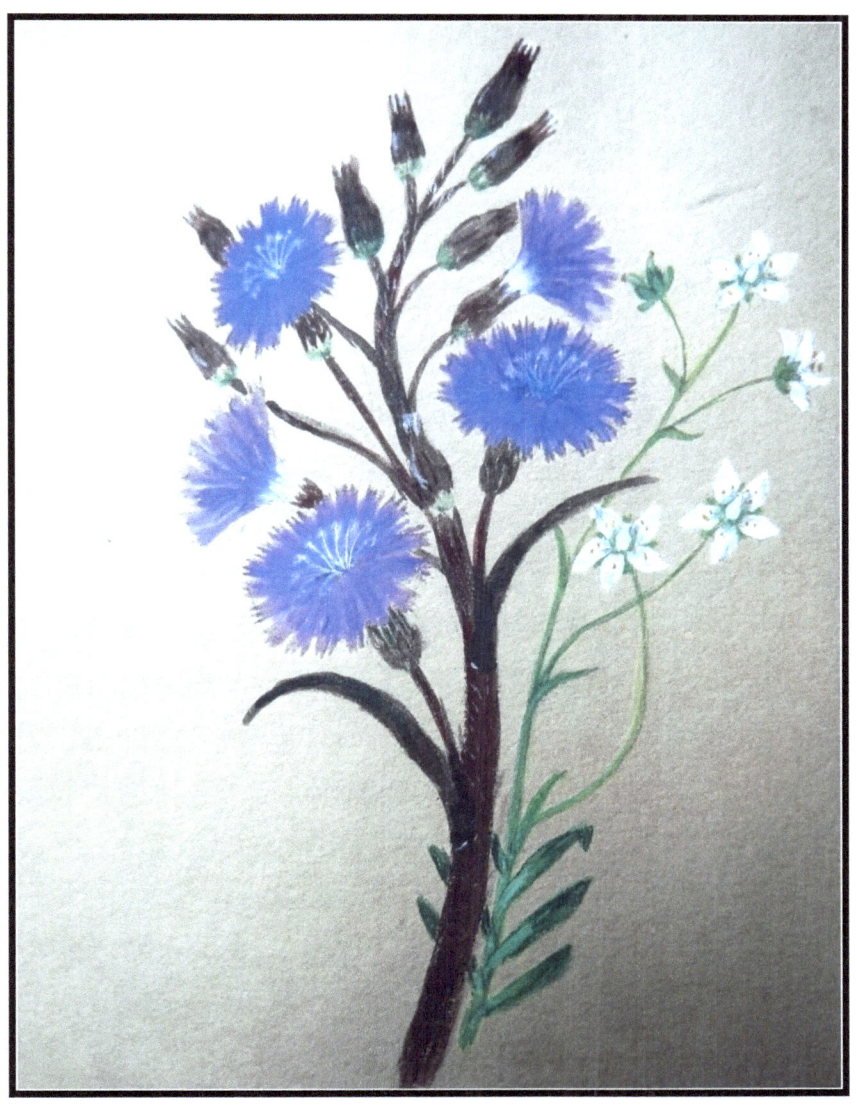

Soldenella [?] - Pontresina, Aug. 20, '77

August 24.

Started directly after breakfast and walked to St. Moritz with friends. Charming day after the rain, dust settled, mountains clear and glaciers sparkling. We took a rowboat across the lake and loitered in the arcades buying pretty things while some of the party took the baths. On the return across the lake, again in a rowboat, [we] went to the falls — very fine — then to the dairy [indecipherable] where we took lunch, looking down upon the lake. Through the woods, home, collecting wildflowers and mosses. I sat down at once to paint them. The red moss was so new and so remarkable to me.

Artwork

[Two Missing Paintings]

On Monday at 8 o'clock with actual tears in my eyes, I bade adieu to the lovely Roseg Glacier. Other friends had parted from us the night before but the glacier was awake and look its brightest. As we drove along, the ground was covered with this autumnal crocus, which springs up after the grass is cut, making a carpet of pink over the fields. We found the Julier Pass not so fearful as the Albula, but also not as majestic. On the top are two pillars, set one on each side of the road, erected by Julius Caesar, who made the road. The terrible Schyn [? Sp.] Pass was passed late, towards night. The precipitous rocks rise thousands of feet above the road and hundreds of feet below roars the river torrent which has in the course of ages formed this gorge. It is well named Via Mala [bad route].

Artwork

[Four Missing Paintings]

July 24th.

I have enjoyed so much this afternoon on our drive to Beaversthal, after painting all the morning. The ground fairly covered with flowers which I gathered beside the babbling, tumbling broke as ravenously as if I had seen no others for a month. There in the wet grass grows the Pinguicula, a water plant but so much like our blue and white violets.

Artwork

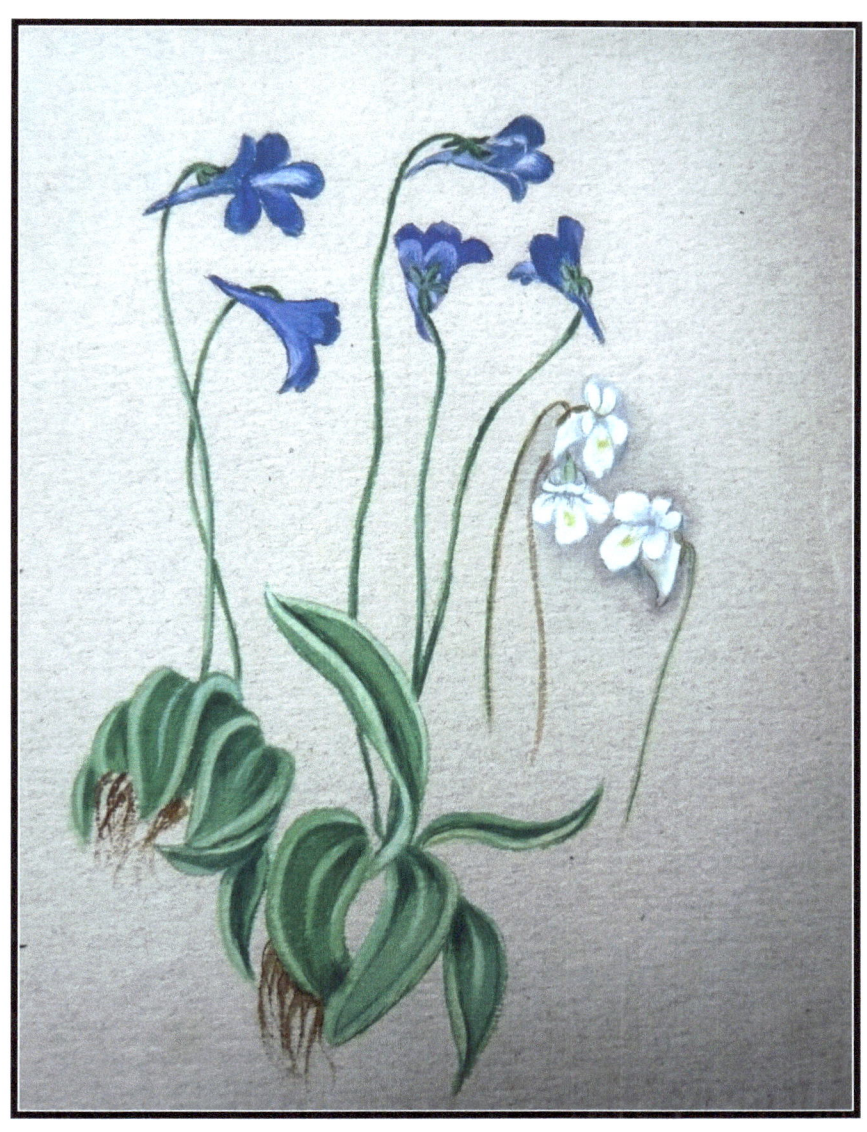

Pinguicula grandiflora
Pinguicula alpine. July 16th, '79

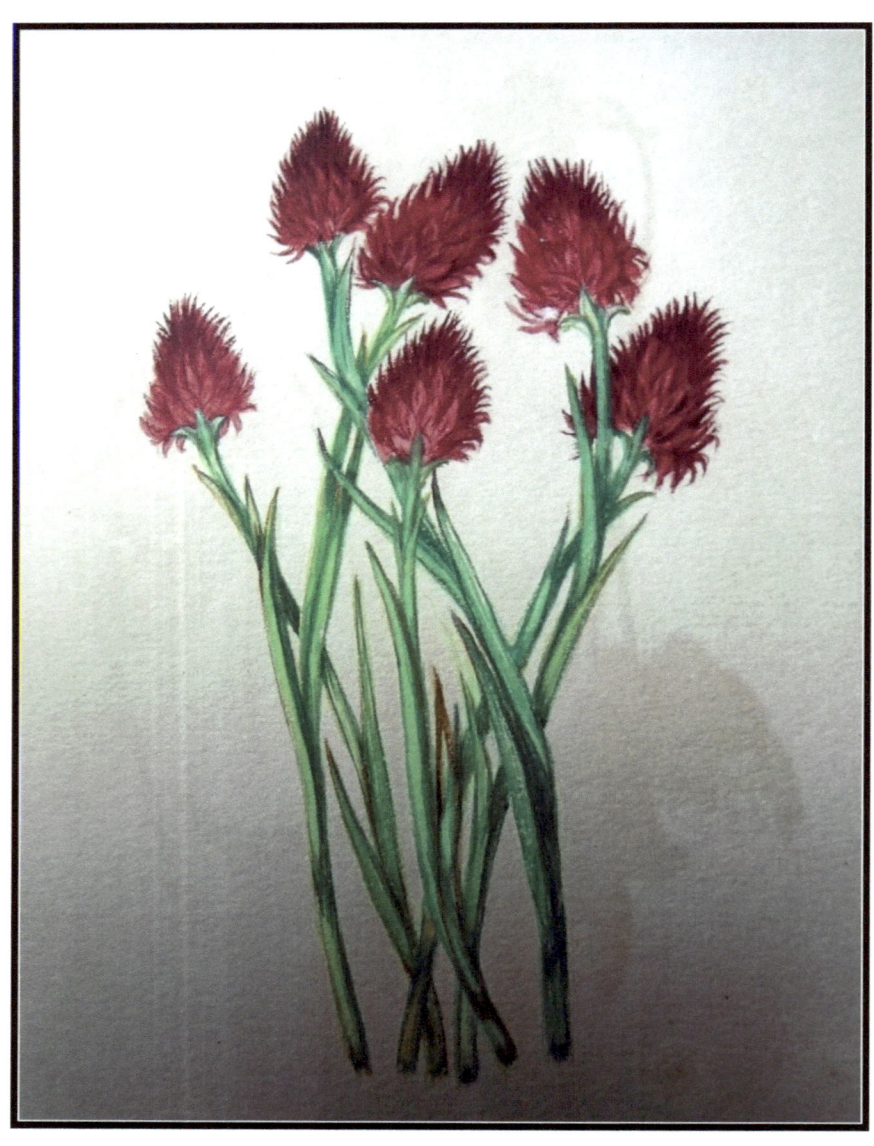

Nigritella Angustifolia, from "Sils Maria". July 17th.

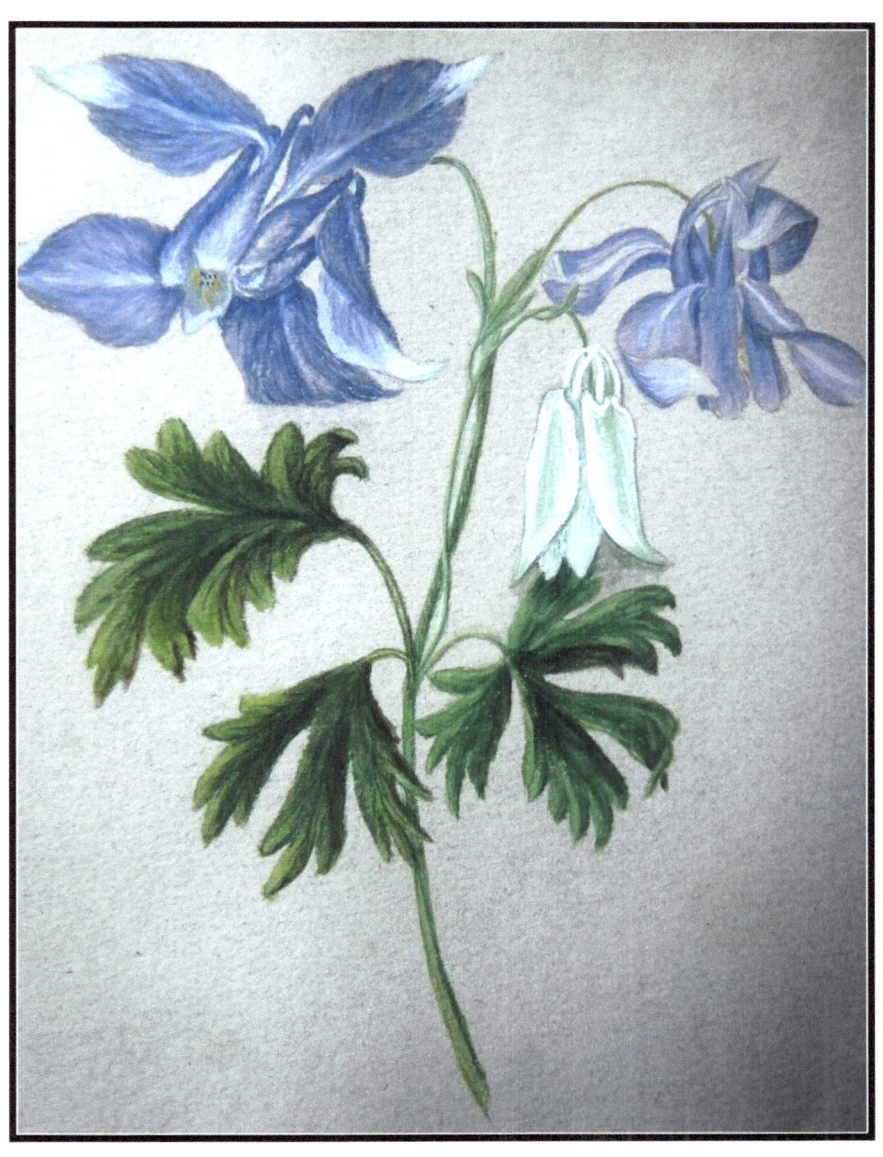

Aquilegia Alpina

From Sils Maria. July 20, 1877

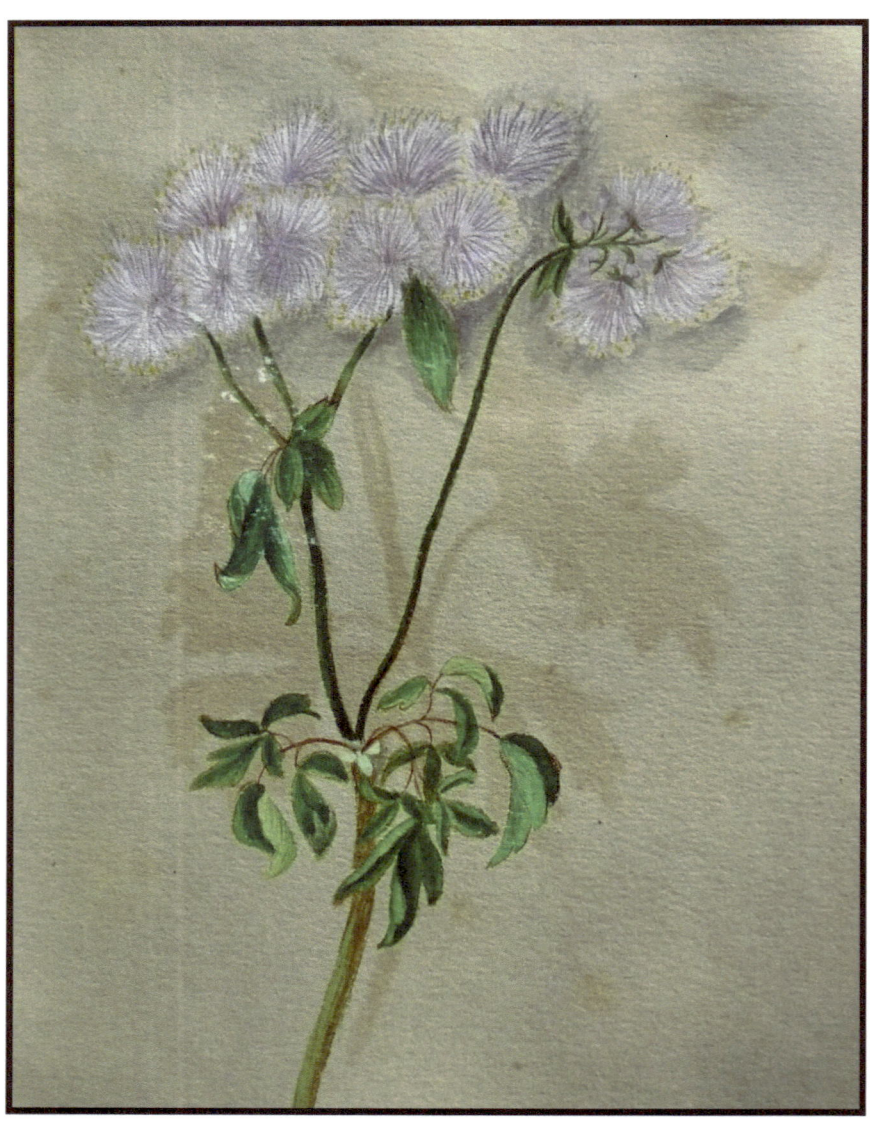

Thalictrum aquilegiifolium. Pontresina. July 21, 1877

Artwork

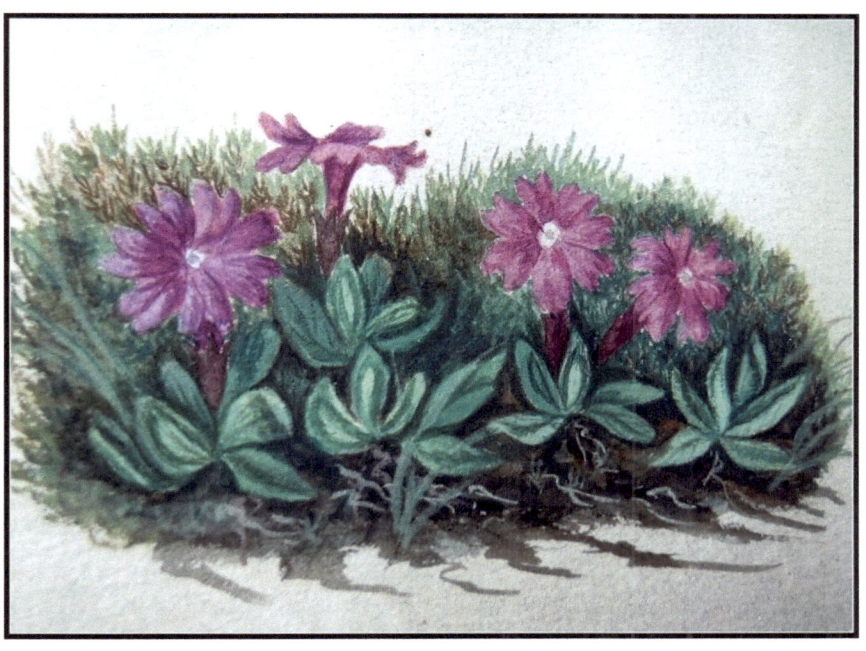

Primula integrifolia. Bernina Pass. July 22, 1879

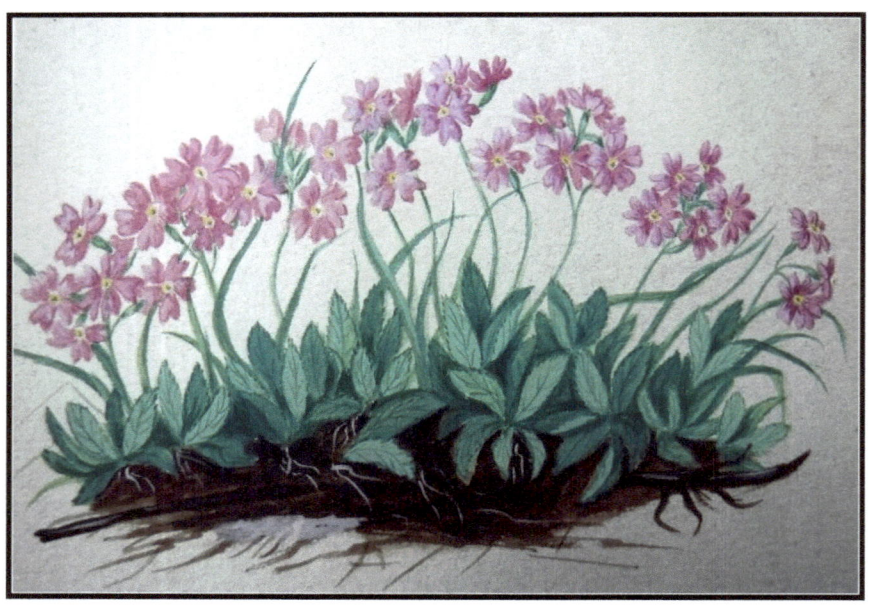

Primula farinose. Bernina Hospice. July 22, 1879

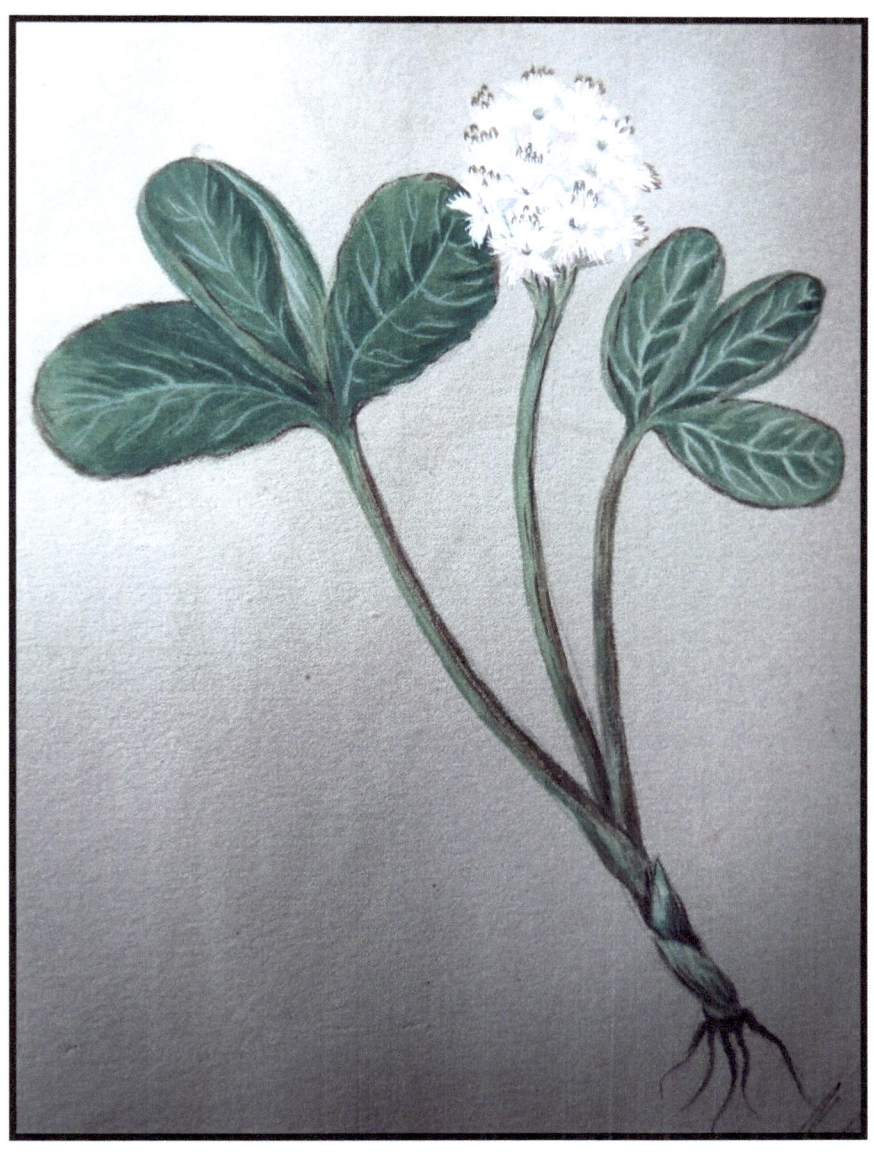

Menyanthes trifoliata. July 26, 1879. Pontresina.

July 15.

Woke this morning to see a severe snow storm. It lay white on the fields. However, this blazing mountain sun dried up the roads by 10 o'clock so that we went for our usual walk. On a scramble up a mountain foot, among the rocks, I found this white Clematis, and a gentleman bought me in the purple one the same day. So I proceeded to paint them forthwith.

Artwork

[Two Missing Paintings]

On Thursday we drove to the Bernina hospice. Delightful drive — views of the Bernina chain of mountains. Could see down into the Italian valley. Ground covered with flowers, as usual. I gathered there the persilla [pusilla] and many gentians, as well as the graceful area like Soldenella.

Artwork

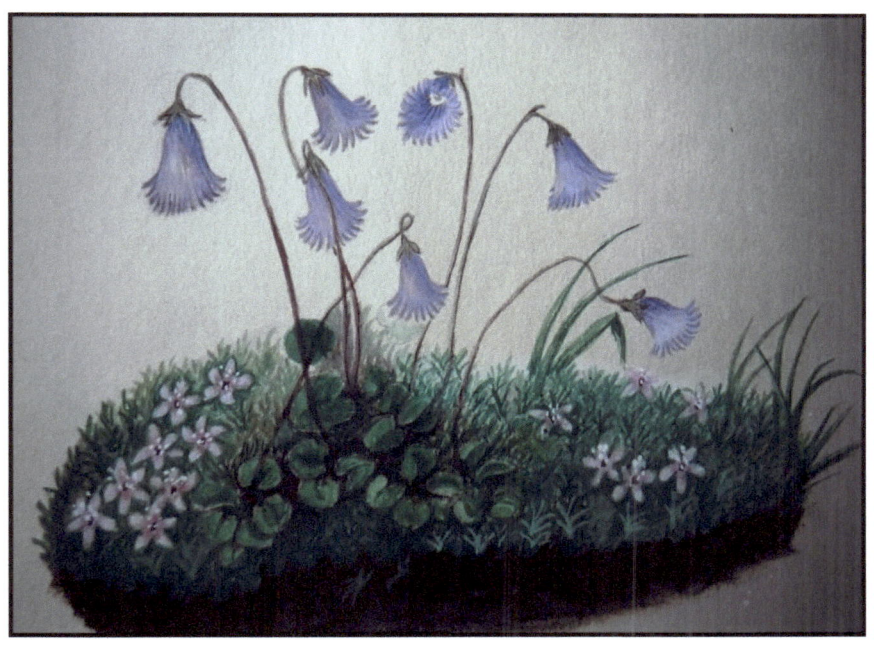

Soldenella persilla [pusilla]   Bernina Pass
   Androsace glacialis   Aug 12, 1879

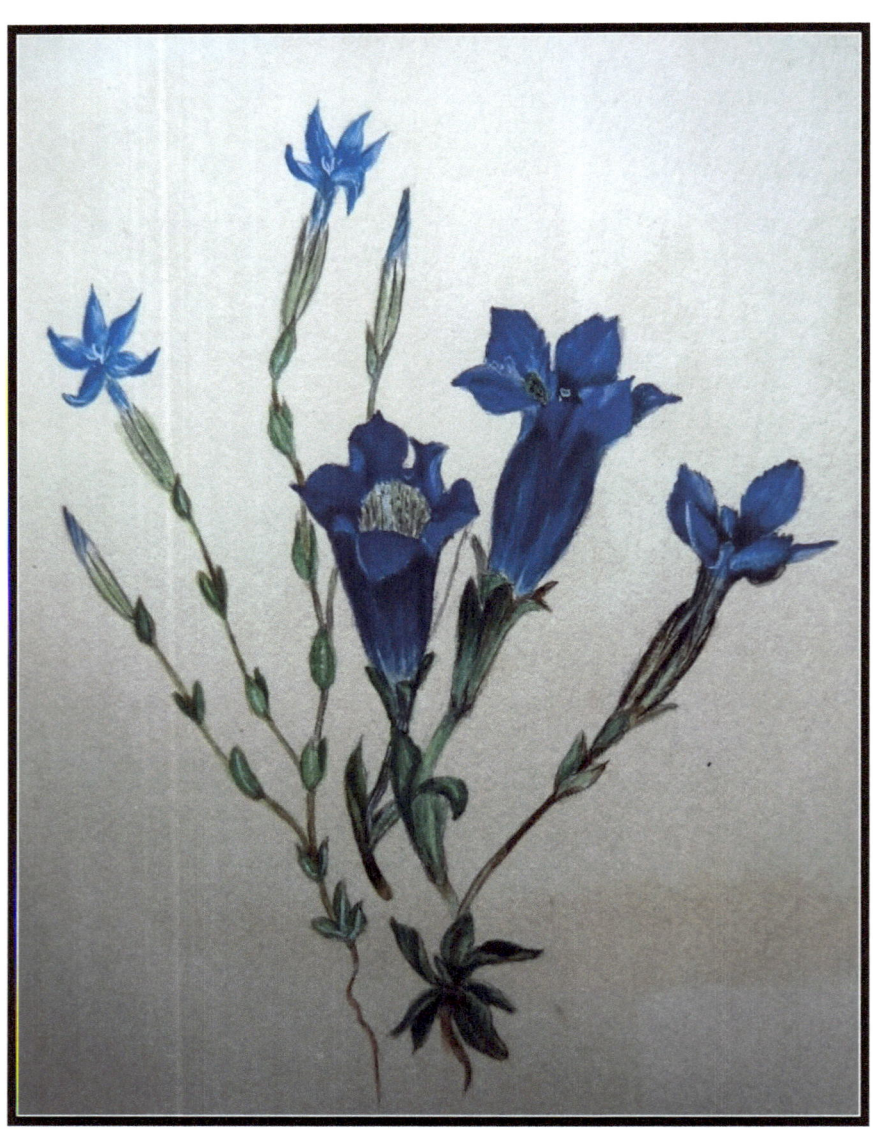

Blue Gentians from Bernina Pass
Aug 13, 1877

Artwork

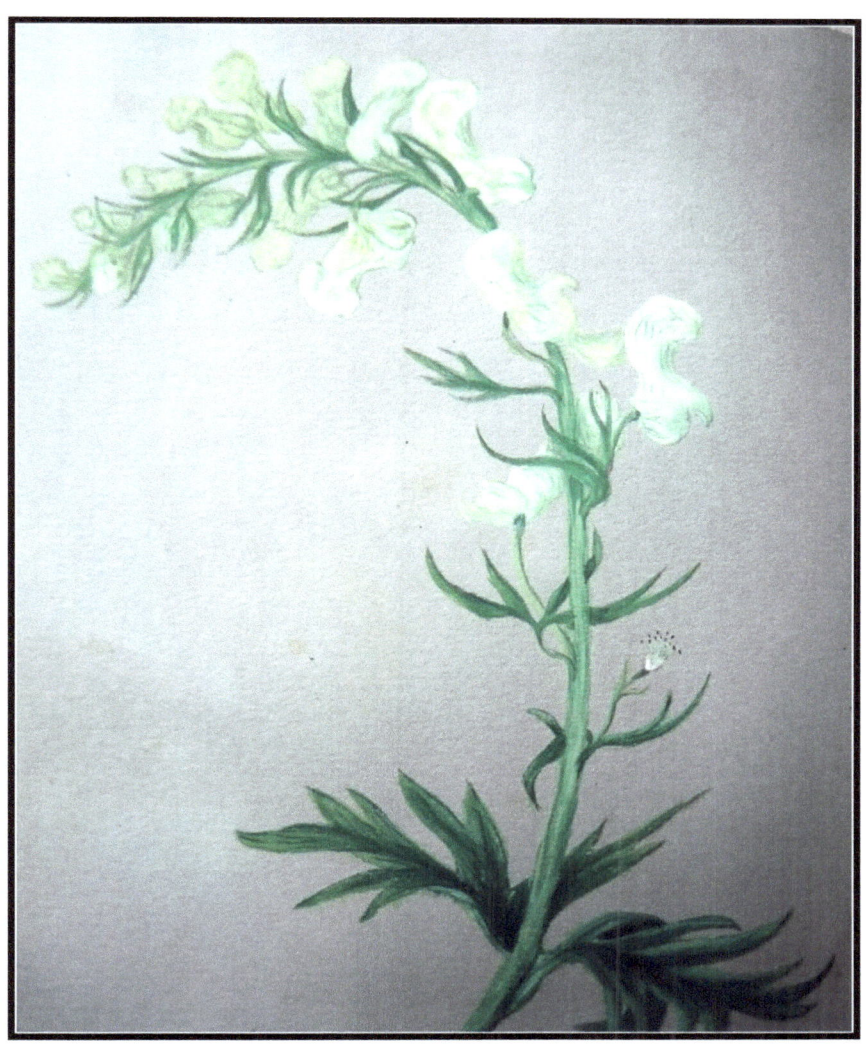

Aconitum lycoctonum   August 15, 1879

Yesterday I painted a thistle which was brought to me by a beautiful young English girl to see if I could make a picture of it. Her father has since been made a Lord. He was one of Gladstone's supporters in parliament. We had many pleasant times with that party — whist in the evening and walks and talks by day.

Artwork

[One Missing Painting]

I seem to be sketching the scenery this summer more than flowers. But I have been determined to get some green flowers, having heard that there were such — and at last I have found some. We had a lovely stroll — I may call it [that], rather than a walk — through the woods to St. Moritz. Took lunch there at the Victoria Hotel and took a [indecipherable] home. Those hotels are more pretentious, but none could be better than our own Roseg here in Pontresina.

Artwork

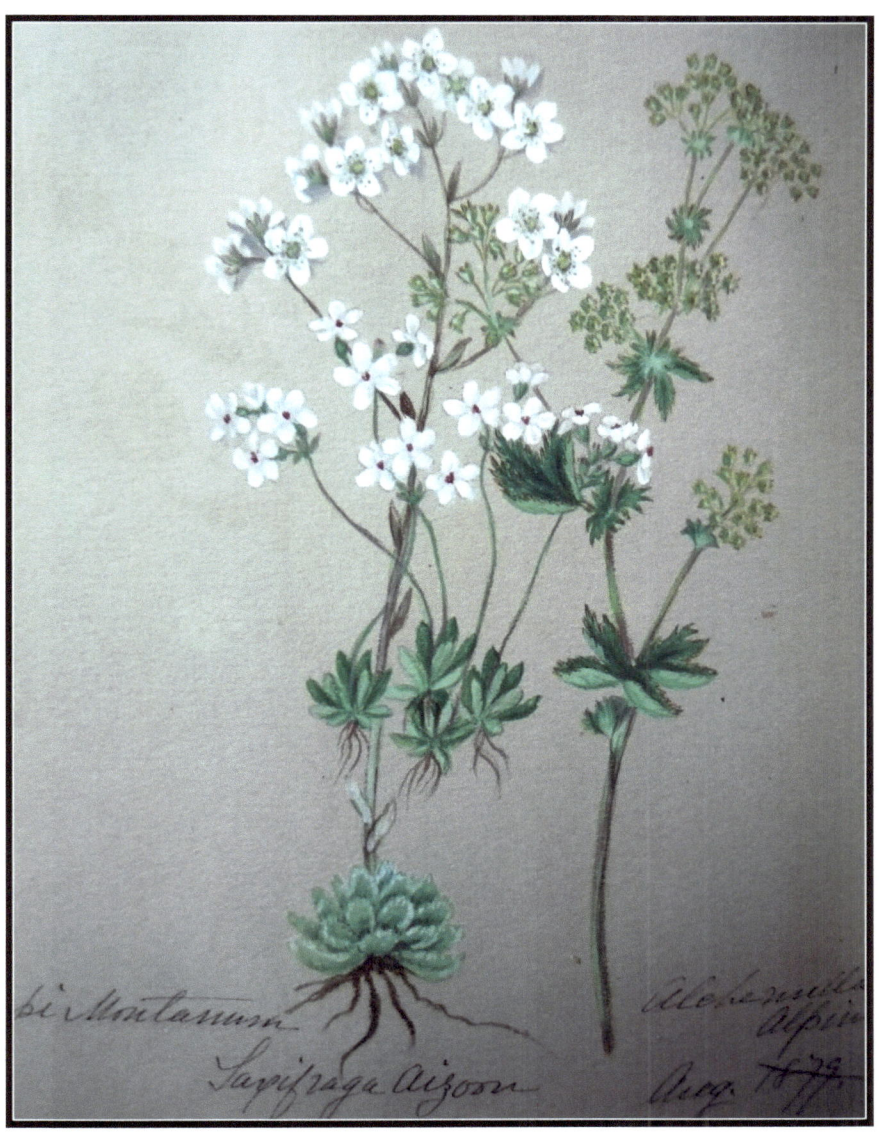

Thlaspi montanum   Alchemilla alpina
  Saxifraga aizoon   Aug 1879

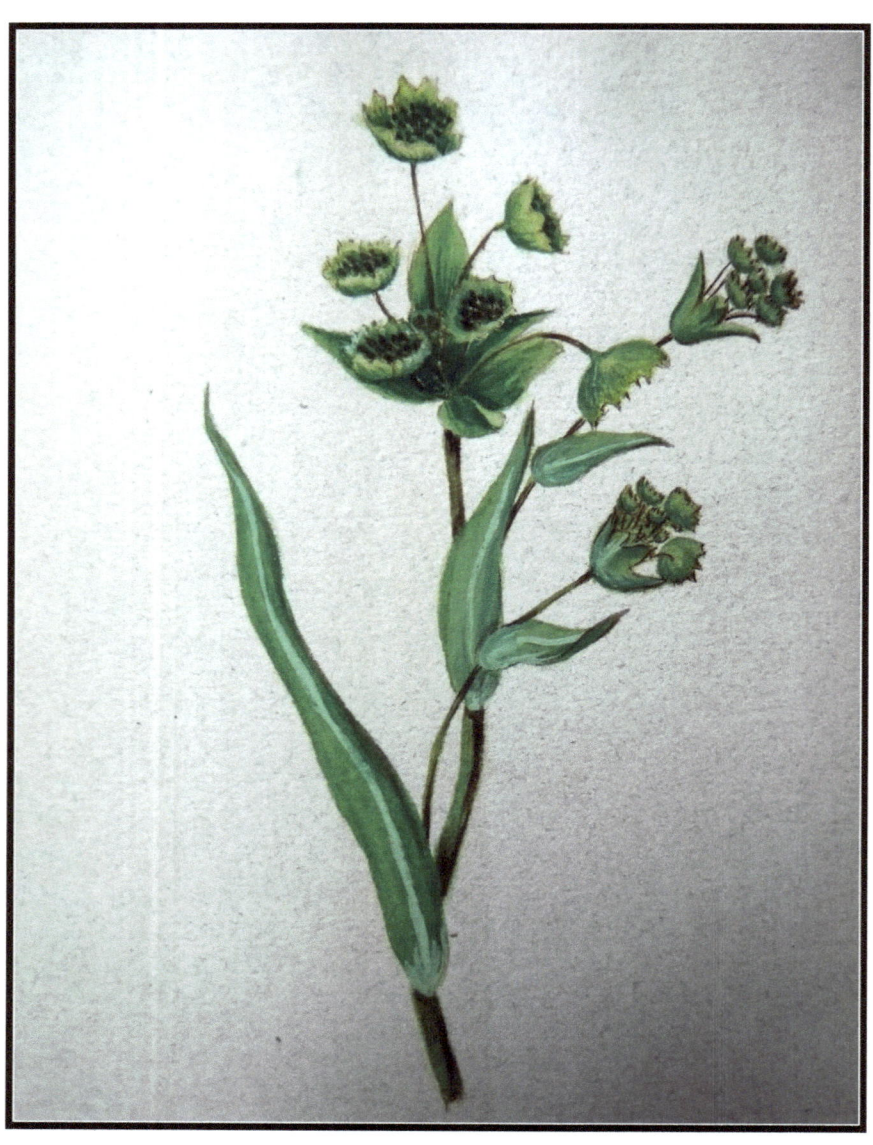

Bupleurum stellatum   Pontresina

Artwork

[One Missing Painting]

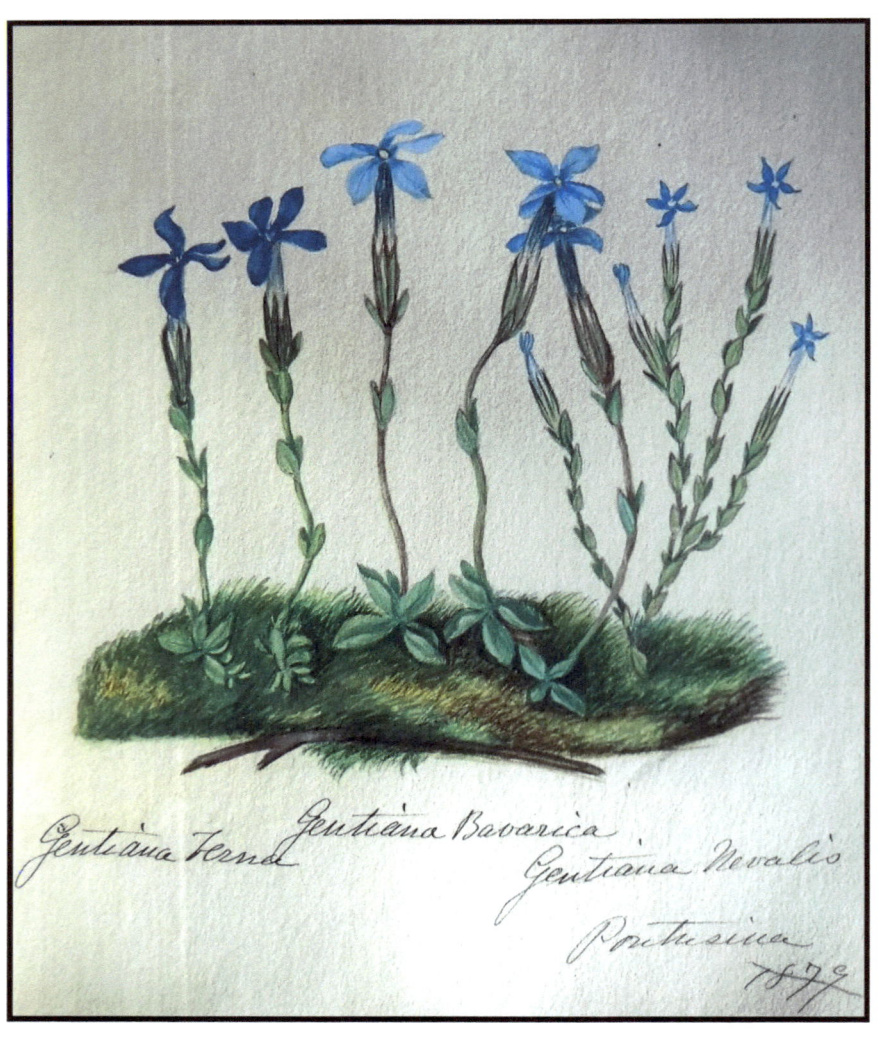

Gentiana Bavarica
Gentiana Verna
Gentiana Nevalis
Pontresina, 1879

August 24 – Davos –

We came from Pontresina yesterday in an extra post carriage – very fine one when we started and paid our 100 Francs – but after luncheon at Sus they changed it for an old one when we began the ascent of the Fluela Pass. Someone had told us [the pass] did not amount to anything. They must have meant the scenery – three mortal hours – I preferred to get out and walk some of the time, and I gathered some flowers. On the top two beautiful little lakes – and flowers – flowers everywhere. I will paint some of them. Here at the hotel Buol we find many agreeable English people. Mr. Symonds – the essayist and poet. He lives here with his family, his lungs compelling him to keep to this air, which is considered specific for consumption. Hundreds of English spend the winter here.

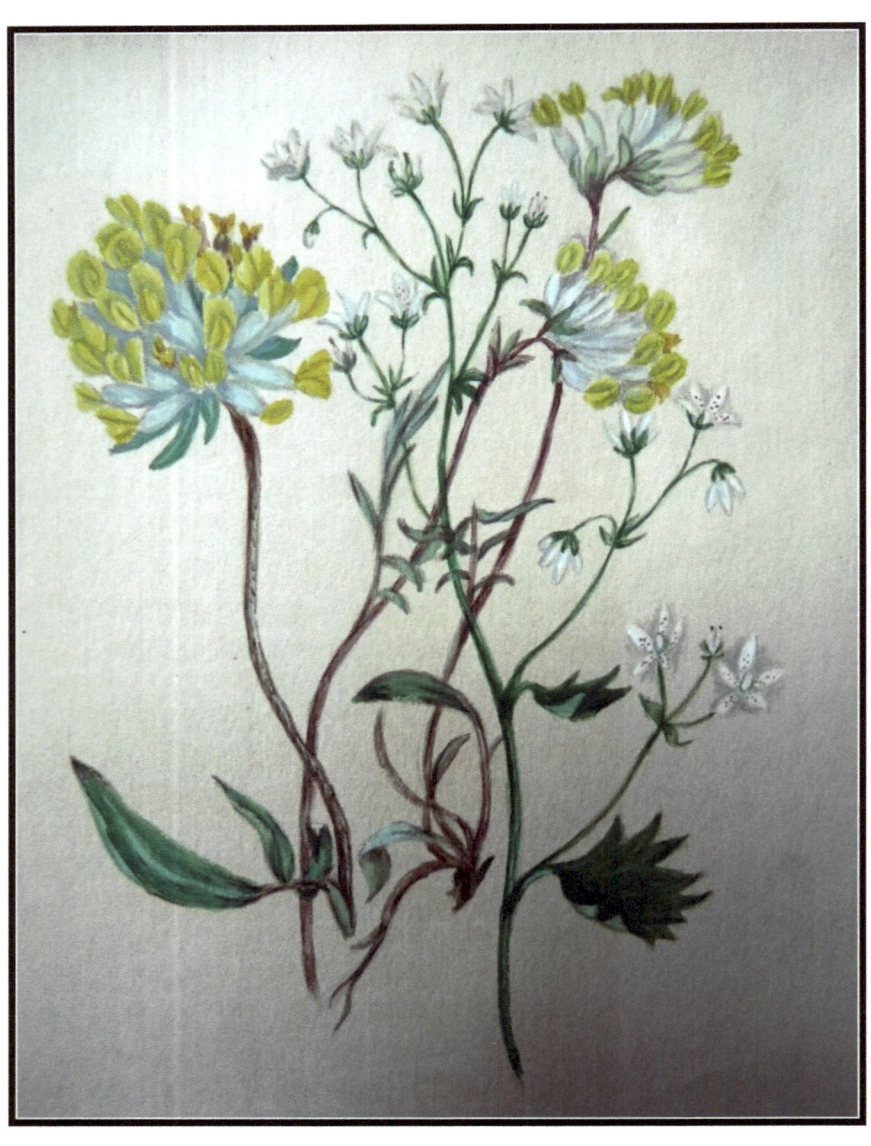

Anthyllis vulneria [vulneraria]

Davos Sept 7, '79

Davos. August 29.

Such a pleasant day — a walk and picnic at Clavadel — about 3 miles and up the mountainside, where we found the gasthof [inn] — a lateral valley opening out of the Davos valley. But not much of the valley, more of a gorge — the river and road at the bottom, one side rising precipitously to a great height and covered with a dark pine forest on the other side. High up above the gorge the hills flatten out into a gentle slope, and there was the gasthof where we took our lunch in a lovely garden full of roses. We had bought some lettuce we saw growing as we came along and the gasthof furnished us with oil, vinegar and coffee. One franc for the party of six! We rambled about on that slope until the afternoon shadows, about 4 o'clock, admitted our walk back to Davos. I was not tired; and went to a play in the evening. Gathered these flowers on the walk.

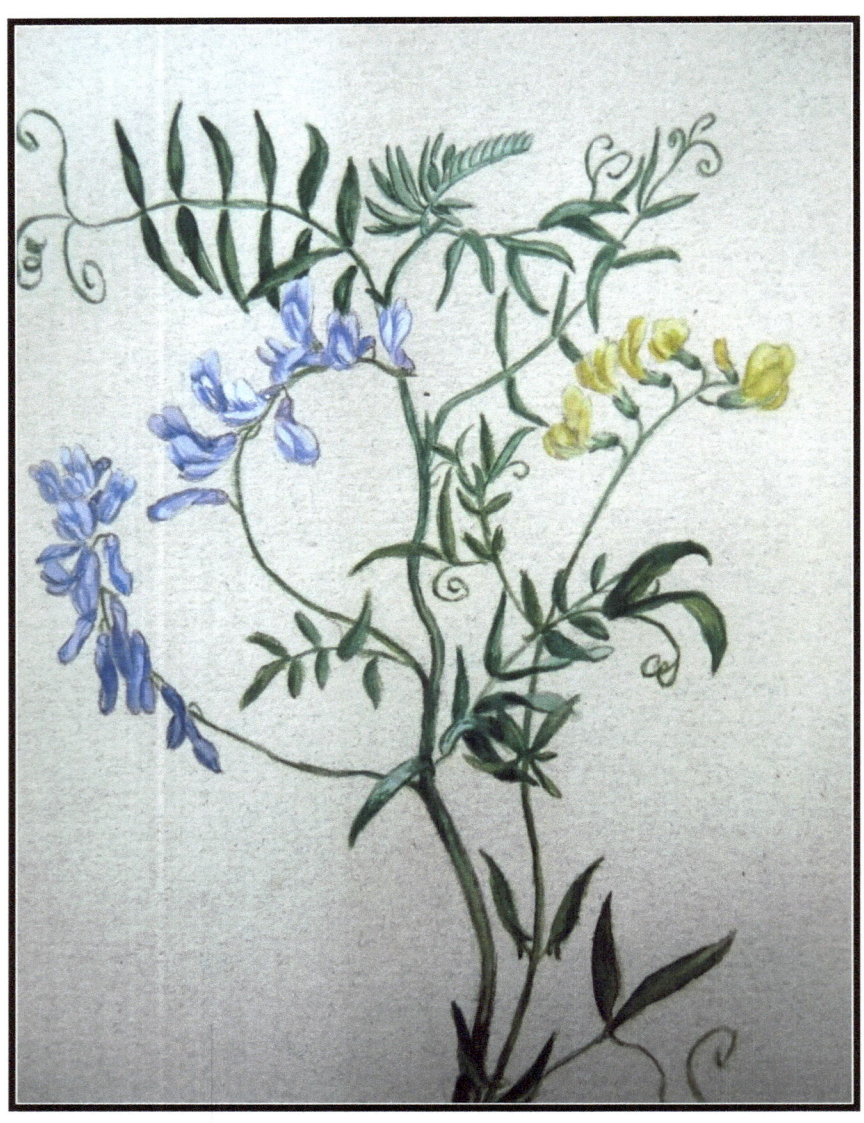

Vicia gracca Lathyrus pratensis
　　　　　　　　Davos, Sept 3, '79

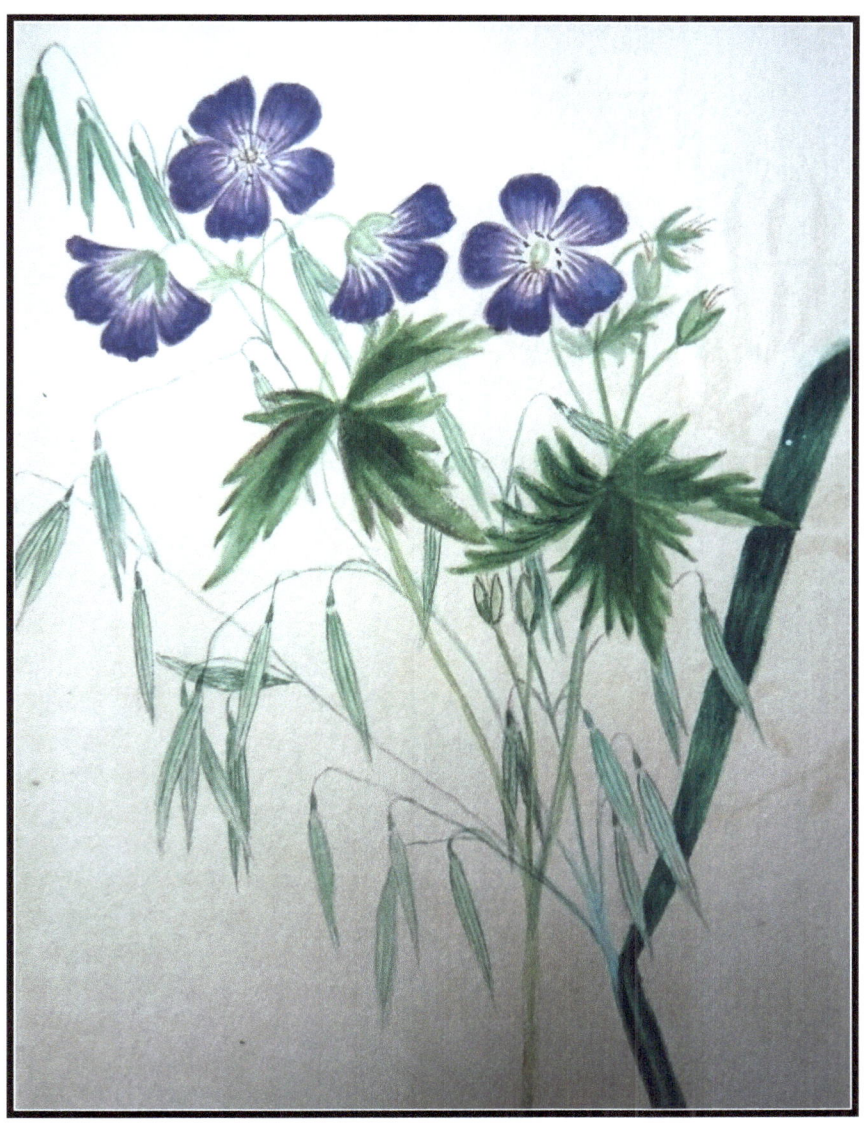

Wild geranium and oats　　　　　Davos, Sept, 13, '79

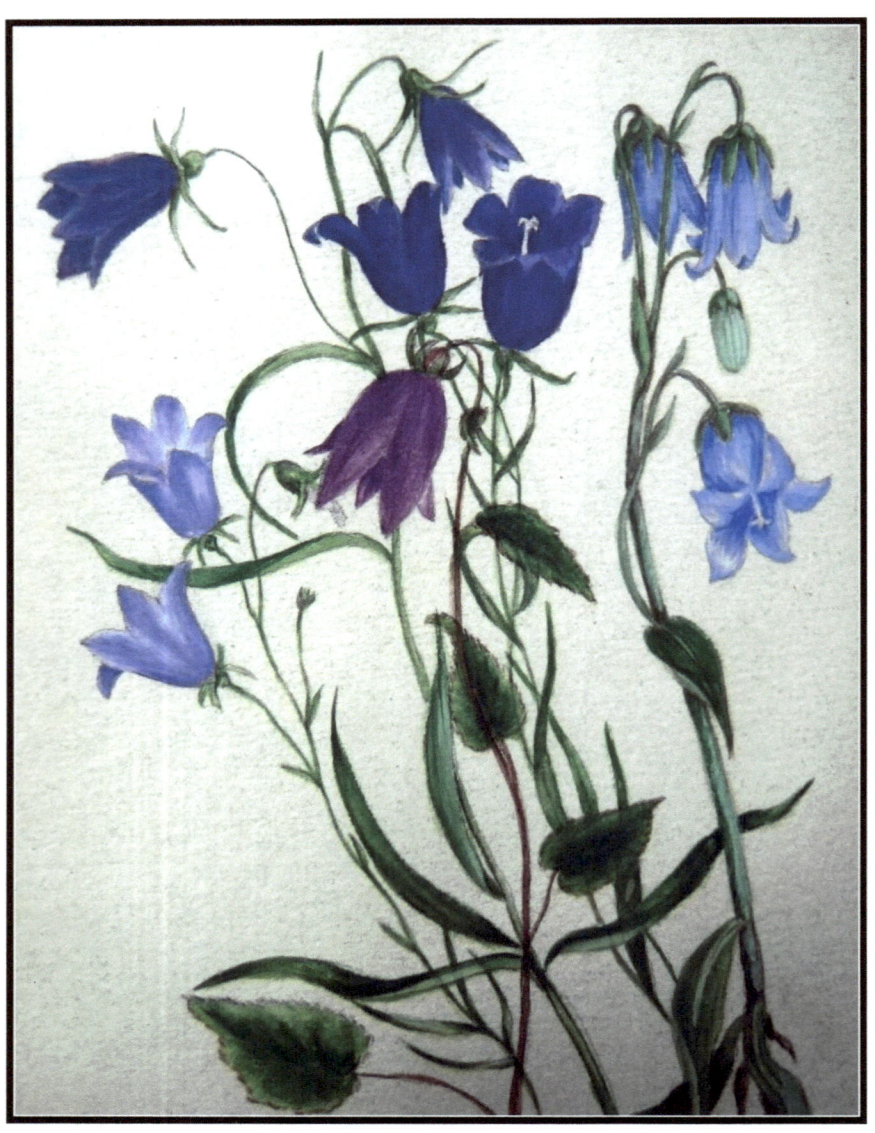

Five varieties of Blue Bells

Davos, Sept 10, '79

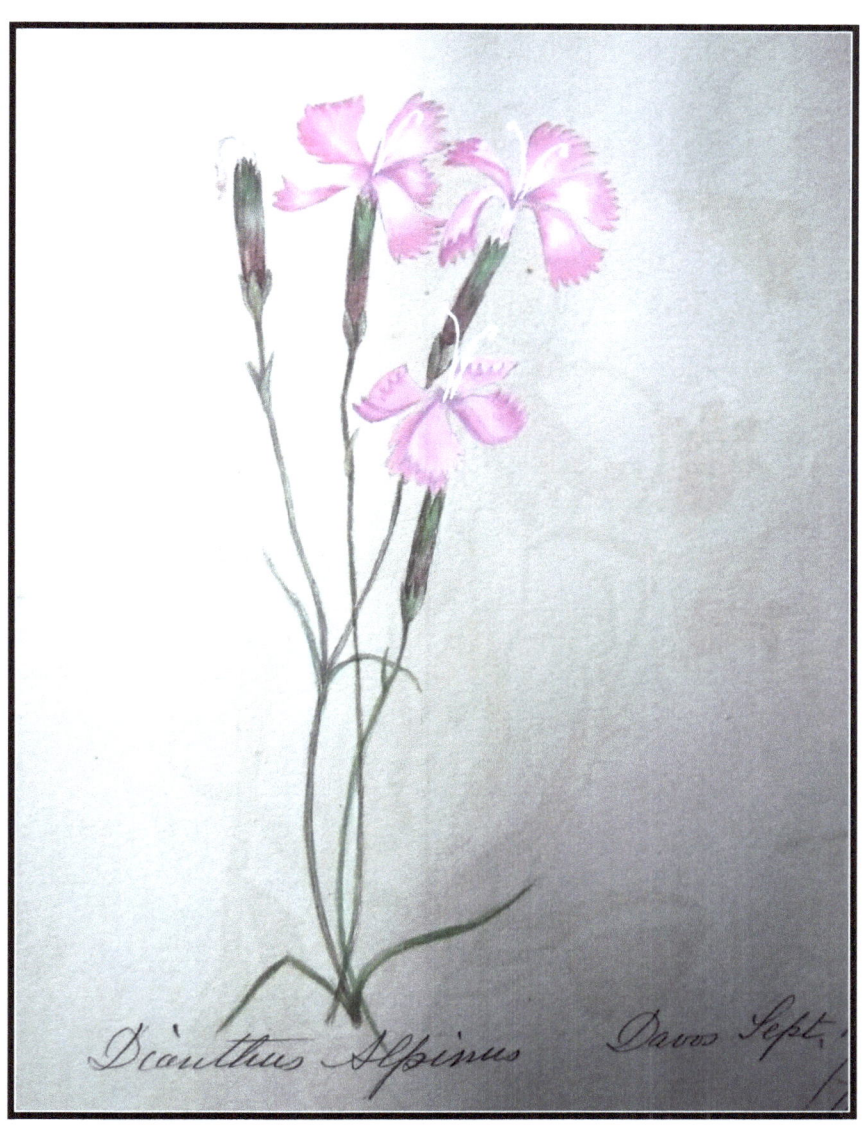

Dianthus Alpina   Davos, Sept 12, '79

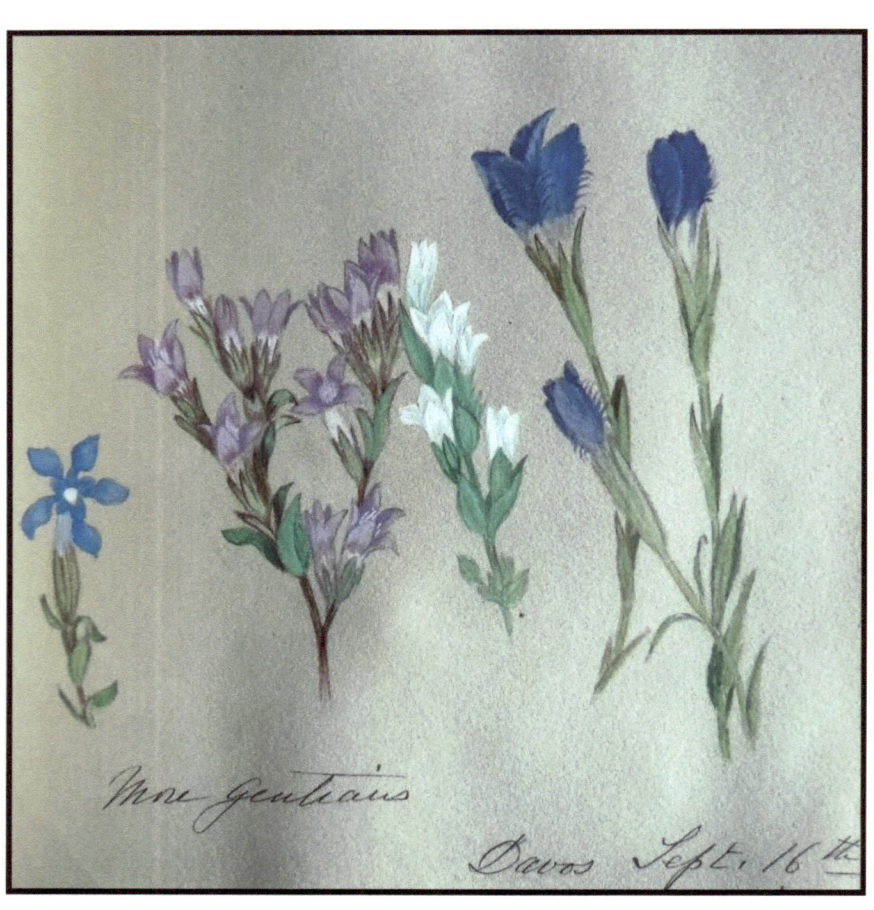

More gentians

Davos, Sept. 16, '79

Landscapes

By

Charlotte W. Throop

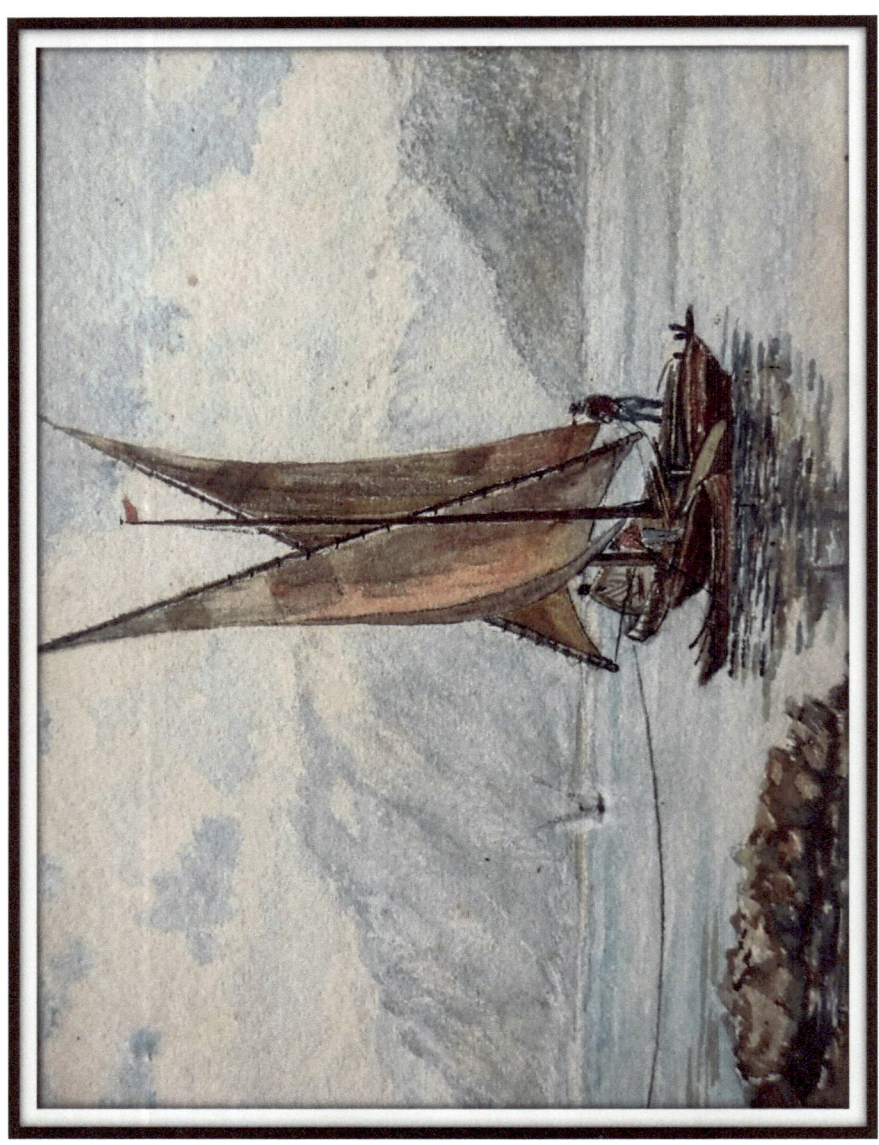

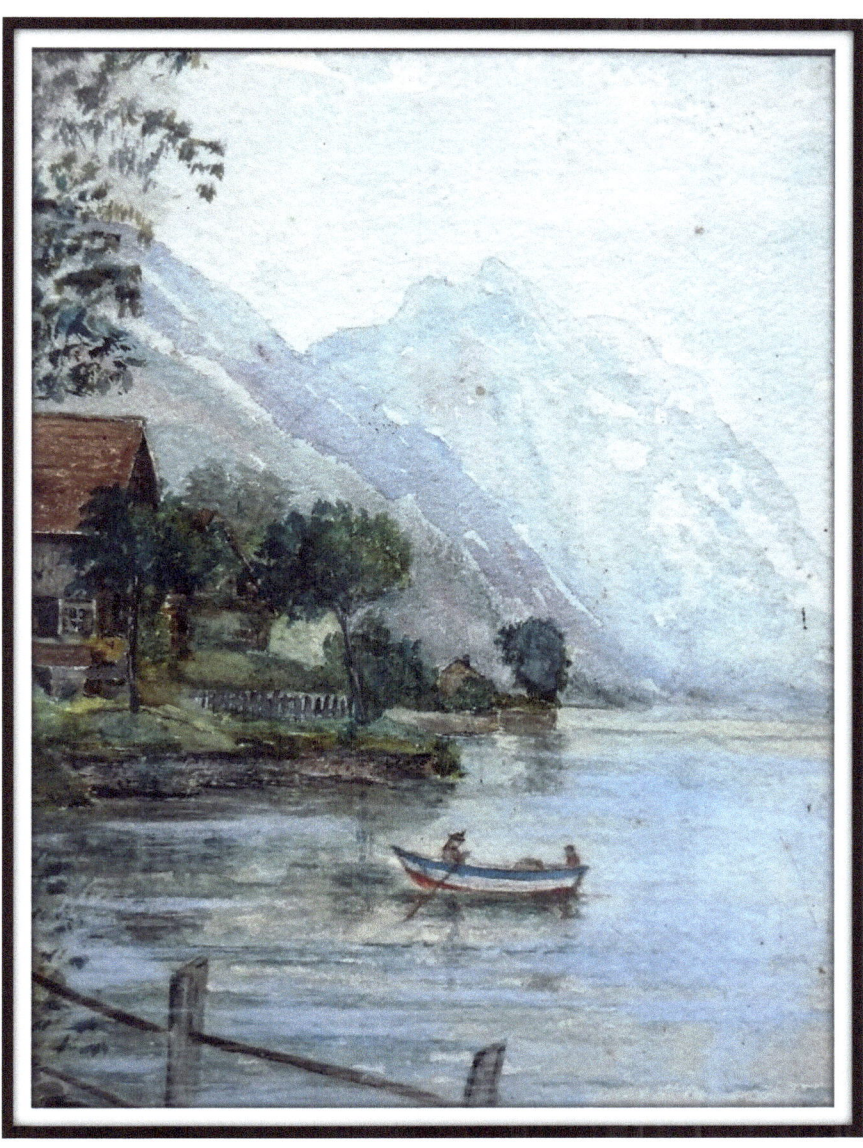

Sketches

By

Montgomery H. Throop (I)

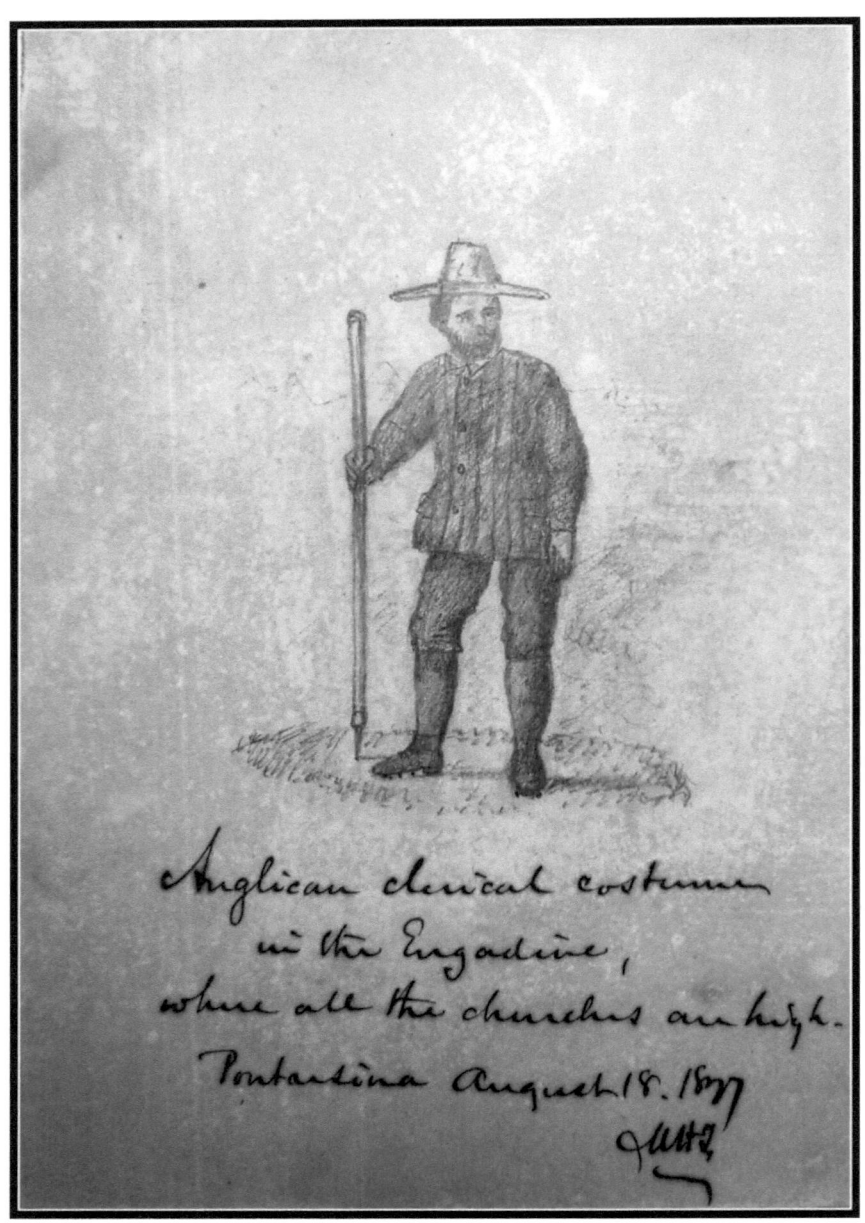

Anglican clerical costume
in the Engadine,
where all the churches are high.
Pontresina August 18. 1897

Artwork

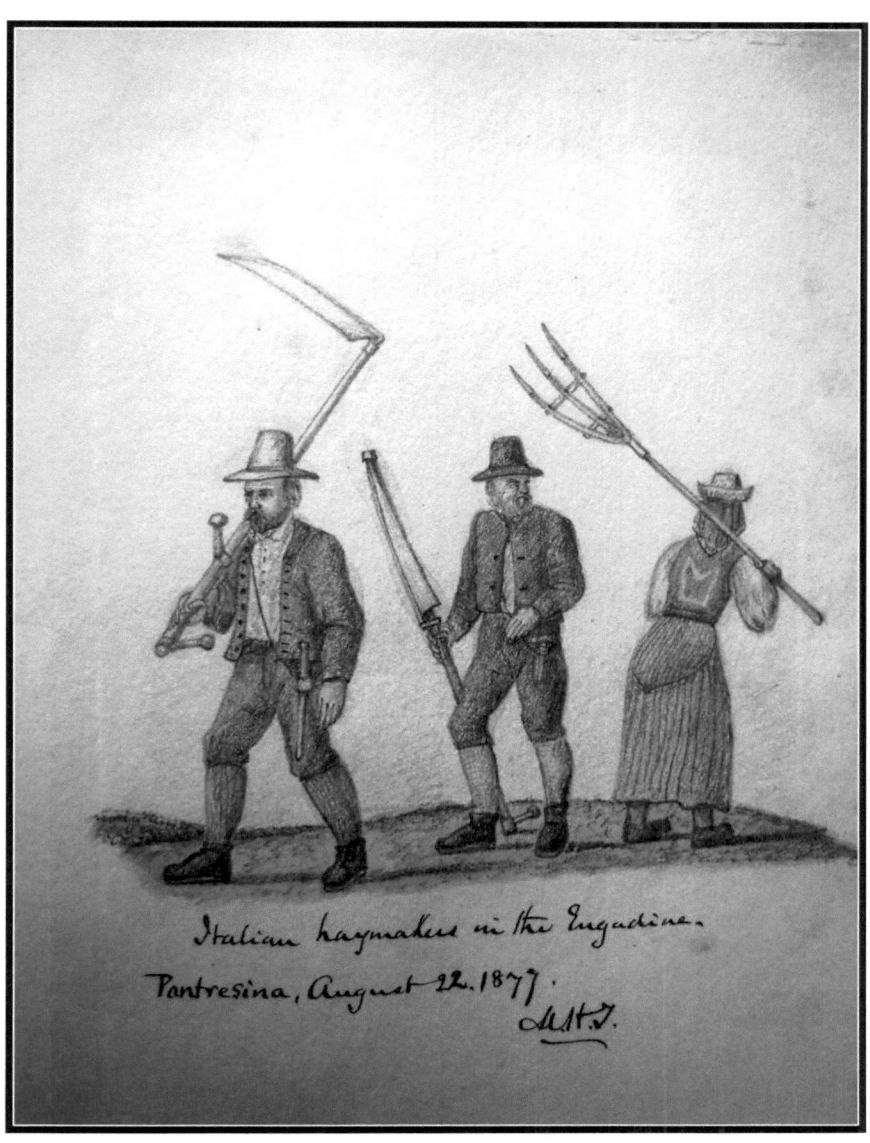

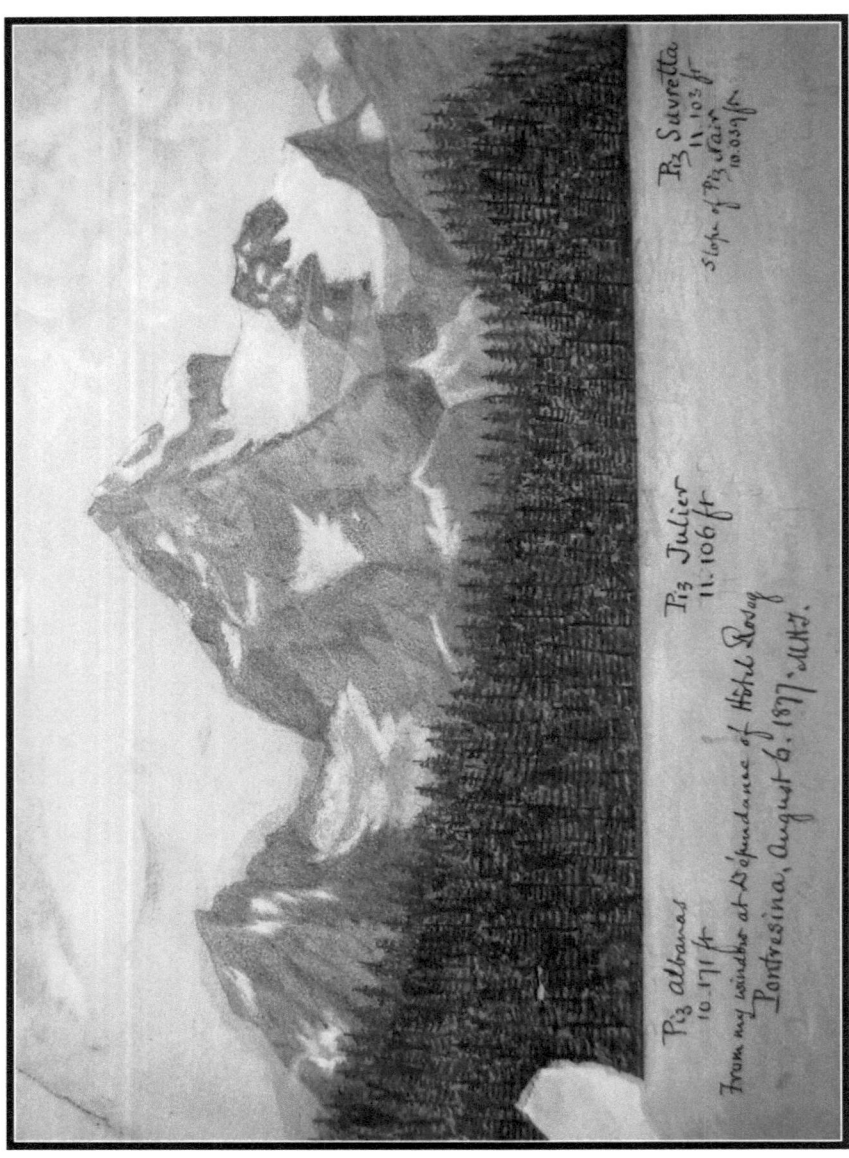

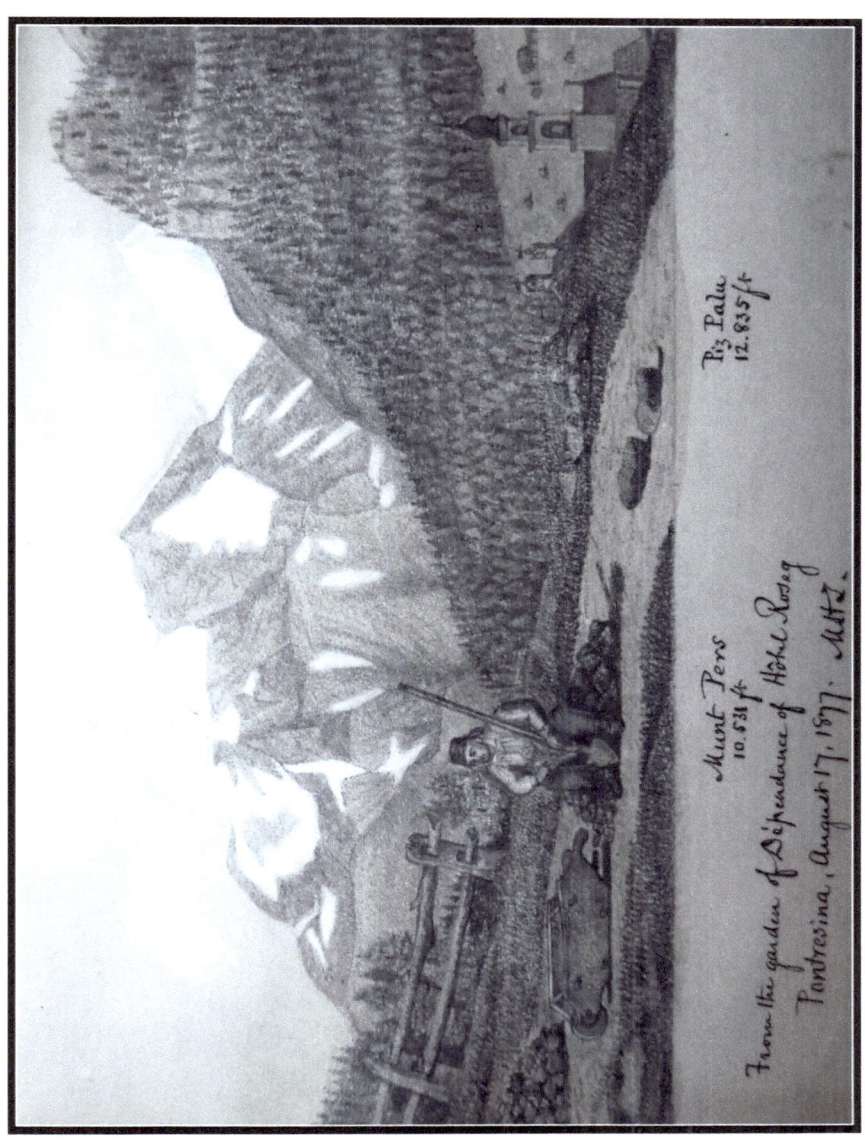

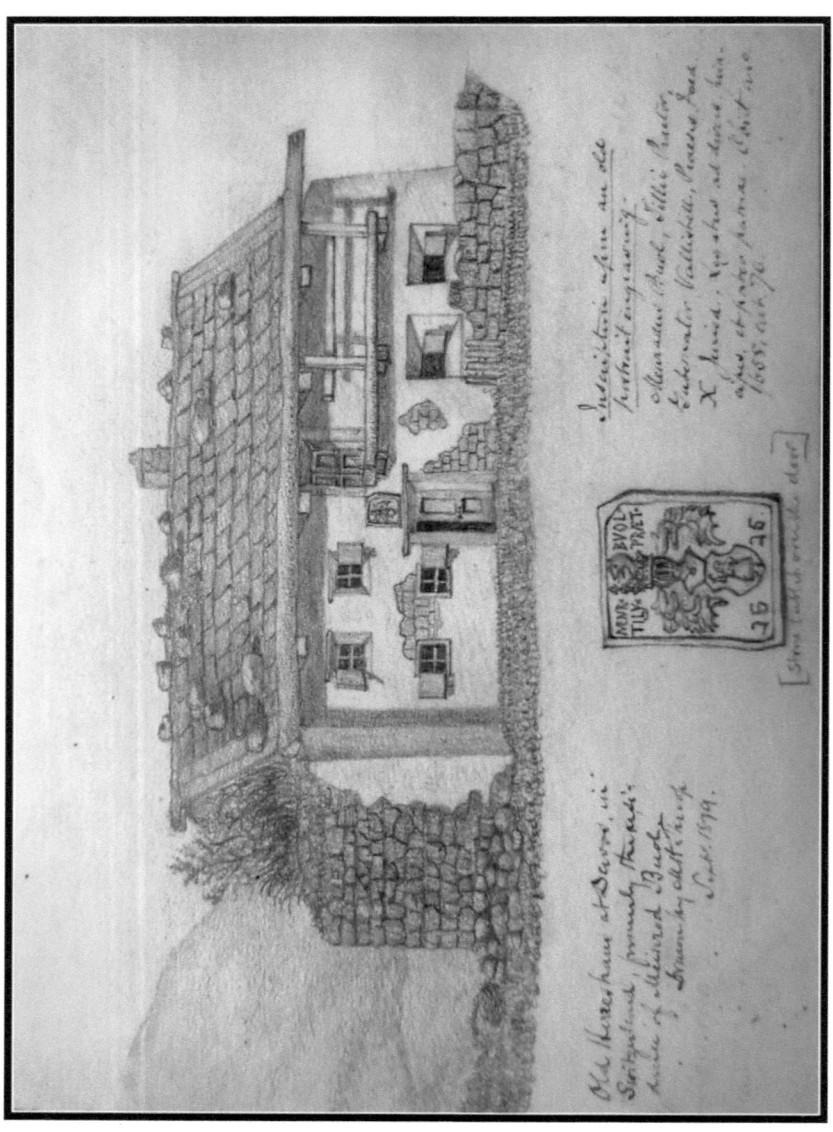

IN APPRECIATION

My mother, Charlotte Throop Shaw

For saving her great grandmother's album.

&

CreateSpace

For providing a venue to share it.

www.ingramcontent.com/pod-product-compliance
Lightning Source LLC
Chambersburg PA
CBHW040223220526
45473CB00001B/102